Praise for
The Resilient Child

"How often have we heard some version of the adage: We are provided no 'owner's manual' when we embark on parenthood! Perhaps Dr Everly and Ms. Brown have rendered that saying out-of-date. In *The Resilient Child*, the authors have woven the best of psychological science, common sense, and personal experience into an eminently readable child rearing guide that is, at once, fundamentally simple and remarkably profound. "

- O. Lee McCabe, Ph.D.
The Johns Hopkins School of Medicine
and The Johns Hopkins Bloomberg School of Public Health

"…This innovative and practical book will assist parents in teaching their children how to cope with stress and adversity and how to develop resiliency…This is not your average book on stress management. In highly original work, Dr Everly discusses topics such as friendship, loyalty, courage, taking responsibility for ones actions, optimism, faith and integrity.

… captivating to read (and) full of engrossing examples, pearls of wisdom and insights. He shares learnings from his personal and professional life that develops an intimacy with the reader. In reading this book I felt at times as though I was sitting with an old friend and sharing innermost thoughts.

…punctuated with lessons, insights, wisdom and understandings …It is a motivational book that can truly help people to change their lives in a profound way. It is also a practical book that is enhanced by exercises that will both help the adult reader to better understand this topic and also assist them in teaching this material to their children…"

- Robyn Robinson, Ph.D., FAPS
Clinical Psychologist, and Founder and President,
Critical Incident Stress Management Foundation of Australia

"Few would argue that our children are under more stress than ever before. They seem to be growing up faster and have little free time for 'just being a kid.' In his latest book, Dr. Everly focuses his expertise on stress and resilience toward young people. He provides the reader with a series of practical, easy-to-follow tips and homework lessons. This delightful and informative book is designed to help busy caregivers and parents guide their children to view their lives as 'half full' even in the face of adversity and the bumps along life's journey."

- Alan M. Langlieb, M.D., MPH, MBA
Director, Workplace Psychiatry, The Johns Hopkins Hospital

"...a book that holds and informs the reader, provides usable information, and challenges all who will read it...there is great wisdom that all can apply and it is the stuff of great personal reflection and family discussion.

...(an) effective blend of research, case presentation, personal experience, disclosure, and passion. Together, these elements build a sound and understandable foundation for the book's major messages. The exercises are a great help to the reader in applying the book's content. All parents who struggle (and that is most all of us) to prepare our children to make the most of their lives and to be good world citizens will find something helpful in this book."

- **Rear Admiral Brian W. Flynn, Ed.D.**
Assistant Surgeon General (USPHS, Ret.)

"Dr. George Everly, Jr., one of the preeminent scholars in the field of stress and trauma, shares some of his vast knowledge of concepts related to areas such as resiliency and personality in this extremely practical and easy-to-read book,... Dr. Everly allows his knowledge as a parent and his heart to serve as the primary inspirational and motivational sources for this book. Its genuineness, passion, and applicability make it a must-read for parents."

- **Jeffrey M. Lating, Ph.D.**
Professor of Psychology, Loyola College in Maryland

"...a rare find; if not a treasure...Dr. Everly offers seven logical lessons that will provide all parents with a useful approach to parenting...These lessons are truly 'gifts' for eternal use...It is simple, direct, and of utmost importance to the children of this world. The gift of resiliency, wrapped in common sense language and everyday lessons, is a wealth of information, a cache of thoughts for consumption. He bares his soul in an effort to teach parents the lessons they owe their children. Lessons that are valued, everlasting, and lessons that will allow them to exist in an ever-changing world, long after they are on their own..."

- **SSA (Ret) James T. Reese, Ph.D.**
Federal Bureau of Investigation, Retired, Founder, Stress Management in Law Enforcement Program, FBI Academy

"...a book that will surely resonate with parents, grandparents, teachers, and anyone responsible for helping to raise a child. This book is not only a collection of important lessons from an internationally known psychologist and psycho-trauma specialist; it is a treasure chest of concrete parent-to-parent advice. This is a book written from the heart of a man who deeply loves his three children...a legacy of practical parenting guidelines to help children to become stress resistant and resilient adults."

- **Jeffrey T. Mitchell, Ph.D.**
Clinical Professor of Emergency Health Services, University of Maryland

"Now HERE is a book of substance. Every parent (EVERY parent) should have a copy in their home. I have had this book exactly 2 days. I have read, re-read, dissected and contemplated this book in an almost fevered frenzy. George Everly has hit it right on the nose. Brilliant ideas and logic. So simple, it's embarrassing that parents (myself included) could not figure this out for themselves…The end result is a resiliency that will help children throughout their lives. I found myself thinking "I totally agree with you" over and over again. It has been exactly 24 hours since my husband and I have begun to institute some of these simple lessons into our children's every day lives. The reaction was almost immediate. Parents who truly want to help their children will have to make the effort every day. My Husband and I are 100% committed to these seven detailed, essential lessons. We are very excited about this book! Kudos to George Everly!! Outstanding insight!"   **- Library Thing Early Reviewer**

"…a wonderfully basic book on raising a well-adjusted and resilient child… gives practical advice you can use to help your own children through life… the homework boxes scattered throughout the book with practical applications were a nice touch. I will be rereading this book as my children grow older."
                                    - Library Thing Early Reviewer

"In a simple, clear and concise manner, this book explains to parents who feel that they are floundering without a manual to raise this little person, that very guide…This is going to be on my list of favorite things to give new parents. I will be sure to tell them that these are the instructions that should have been included at birth."   **- Library Thing Early Reviewer**

"…packs a ton of great and useful information within its pages, information that one can come back to again and again. In the beginning, Dr. Everly expresses the fact that this book is written as a gift to his children. The gift of resiliency that they can take with them anywhere, throughout their entire lives. It is not necessarily the book itself that is the gift, but the true treasure of lessons that it holds between it's covers. Now, through The Resilient Child, Dr. Everly, Jr. is kind enough to bestow this gift to all of us and what a true gift it is."
                                                    - Café of Dreams

"…gives parents and caregivers a blueprint of how to rear a child who is more aware and able to better handle the many adversities of life…Throughout the book are "homework" sections that sometimes give examples or "what if" situations that the adult and child can discuss together…you may find yourself becoming a better and more complete person as you strive to teach your children how to live a life with less stress and grow to become positive individuals who happily reach their full potential…"
                                    - Library Thing Early Reviewer

THE
RESILIENT
CHILD

Seven Essential Lessons
for Your Child's Happiness
and Success

GEORGE S. EVERLY, JR., PH.D.
The Johns Hopkins University Bloomberg School of Public
Health
Center for Public Health Preparedness
Loyola College in Maryland
and
The Johns Hopkins University School of Medicine

with
SLOANE BROWN

DiaMedica Publishing
150 East 61st Street
New York, NY 10065

Visit our website at www.diamedicapub.com

Library in Congress Cataloging in Publication data:
Available from the Publisher on request.

ISBN: 978-0-9793564-5-2

Editor: Jessica Bryan
Book Design: Janice St. Marie

To my children: Marideth, George, and Andi.

I pray that someday you will be lucky enough
to have children who will teach you
as you have taught me and bring you the happiness
that you have brought me.
But most importantly, I pray your children
will show you the love that you have shown me.

And just remember:
Happiness is a journey, not a destination, so never stop trying!

Acknowledgments

I have already mentioned my three children, Marideth, George, and Andrea (Andi), but I must also thank my parents George S. Everly, Sr. and Kathleen Webster Everly, who created the foundation for this book.

I also thank the many physicians and psychologists who have supported me and taught me what I know about resilience: Douglas Strouse, Steven Sobelman, Jeffrey Mitchell, Lee McCabe, James T. Reese, Michael Kaminsky, Jon Links, Brian Flynn, David McClelland, Theodore Millon, Daniel Girdano, Bert Brown, Terrie Elliott, Cindy Parker, Stan Platman, Russell Hibler, Susan Townsend, and Jeffrey Lating.

Thanks also to Charles Nemphos, Don Howell, Elmer and Alma Schabdach, L. E. and Dorothy Kielman, Robert and Connie Newman, and, of course, Carol Kielman and Gayle Schabdach, with whom this journey began.

GEORGE S. EVERLY, JR., PH.D.
JULY, 2008

About the Authors

GEORGE S. EVERLY, JR., PH.D., is a leading expert in the field of stress management. His books *Controlling Stress and Tension* and *A Clinical Guide to the Treatment of the Human Stress Response* are considered academic classics. Dr. Everly currently serves on the faculties of The Johns Hopkins University School of Medicine, The Johns Hopkins Center for Public Health Preparedness, The Johns Hopkins University Bloomberg School of Public Health, and Loyola College in Maryland.

As one of the "founding fathers" of modern resiliency and stress management, Dr. Everly has identified and synthesized the common denominators required for success in these areas. In his role as a mental health advisor in the wake of mass disasters such as the Oklahoma City bombing, Hurricane Andrew, Hurricane Katrina, the devastation of Kuwait after the Iraqi invasion, the terrorist attacks of 9/11, and SARS, he has gained a unique perspective on how human beings react in highly stressful situations. Dr. Everly is uniquely qualified to offer insight into the nature of human resiliency in the wake of extreme adversity, and has now applied this expertise to the development of resiliency in children, so that they will better be able to deal with life's adversities.

SLOANE BROWN has worked in media for 30 years as a disc jockey, news announcer, and news director in radio, and as a daily news reporter, news anchor, and arts reporter/critic in television. Since 1999, Sloane has been the society/party reporter for *The Baltimore Sun*.

She has been married to clinical psychologist Dr. Steve Sobelman for 23 years, and has become an expert in translating "psychology-speak" into layman's terms. Sloane is delighted to use these skills in helping Dr. Everly transition from the lectern to the living room.

Preface

Did you ever hear anyone say, "If only I had known then what I know now"? Well that's the story of my life, a life of constant discovery. Sometimes the "discoveries" came later than I would have liked, but I guess better late than never, right? This book is about a journey of discovery. Its content was shaped by various events that have occurred throughout my lives as student, teacher, researcher, clinician, and parent. But most of all it was shaped by the greatest discovery I ever made—my kids.

Through most of my career, I have specialized in the treatment of stress-related illnesses—anxiety, depression, mid-life crises, as well as headaches, high blood pressure, ulcers, and post-traumatic stress. People even came to be treated for "burnout" (psychological and sometimes physical exhaustion)—job burnout, marital burnout, parental burnout—you name it! It finally dawned on me that many of these individuals, through no fault of their own, were not very resilient—they had a minimal ability to cope with stress. I also realized that learning how to be resilient, learning how to cope with stress, was a life skill that might have prevented, or at least greatly reduced, their need for treatment as adults. If only they had learned resiliency earlier in their lives. What a simple concept—teach children how to be stress resilient!

What is resiliency and why is important? *Resiliency is the acquired immunity against disabling stress.* It is the ability to rebound from adversity. It is an inner strength that increases the likelihood of success in anything you do. One of the foundations of resiliency is the belief in your own personal effectiveness. It is the belief in your ability to organize and carry out the actions required to achieve the things you need and want in life. This perception of personal effectiveness, control, or influence, is an essential aspect of life itself. People guide their lives by their beliefs of personal effectiveness.

Our kids live in a stressful world! The pressure to be well-liked, to be attractive, get high grades in order to get into the "right" schools, all seems worse than it was when I was growing up. The media bombards our children with the sights and sounds of "success," but at what cost? A substantial percentage of young girls want to be thinner, four-fifths of 10-year-olds are afraid of being fat, and anorexia is the third most common chronic illness among adolescents. How about violence? Eighty-six percent of public schools experienced incidents of crime in 2005–2006. Preteen and teenage girls have the highest level of suicide seen in fifteen years, and suicide is the third leading cause of death for all adolescents. If any group of children ever needed resiliency, this one is it!

Many years ago, I was invited to give a lecture at the FBI Academy. The topic of my presentation was stress. I had received a great education. I knew all the principles. I knew all the techniques. I had written books on the subject. My presentation was well-received.

What followed was an amazing lecture by Supervisory Special Agent Dr James Reese on stress in law enforcement. He said something that has stayed with me to this day: "Make a promise to never do anything that will reflect poorly on your parents, your spouse, or your children." Those words hit me like "a ton of bricks." The words were so simple, yet so powerful.

I was annoyed—why hadn't someone told me that earlier in my life? Then I *really* got annoyed—why hadn't *I* thought of that?

Many years later, while I was thinking about estate planning and the material things I wanted to leave my children, I began also thinking of what I could give my children, beyond material things, that would benefit them long after my death. I thought I could teach them all the stress management techniques I had learned throughout my career. But I thought I should say more. I wanted to give them something that would not only help them rebound from the stressful life events they would encounter, but that would give them a little bit of "immunity" from the stress of living. Then, like a laser cutting through a dark night, it hit me. I thought of the many "challenging" questions my children had asked as they were growing up. I remembered the words I had heard at the FBI Academy. I then knew the gift I should try to give my children—resiliency—the same resiliency that many of my patients did not have!

The question was, could I develop a set of guidelines or recommendations that would help my own children develop resiliency? So, I tried. As I developed the concepts and recommendations, I began including them in my lectures. Invariably, people would say how much they enjoyed my remarks on resiliency, and some even asked for the slides I had shown. This response led me directly to the writing of this book.

Our journey to understand resiliency consists of seven lessons that I believe you can teach your children and, in doing so, can help them build the true inner strength that is resiliency.

- Develop strong relationships with friends and mentors.
- Learn to make difficult decisions.
- Learn to take responsibility for your own your actions.
- Learn that the best way to help others, and yourself, is to stay healthy.
- Learn to think on the bright side and harness the power of the self-fulfilling prophecy.
- Believe in something greater than you are.
- Learn to follow a moral compass: Integrity.

I have come to agree with the concept that our lives are defined, and our legacies shaped, not by what we acquire in our lives, but by what we pass on to others. This book will help shape your legacy. It is about giving to others. More specifically, it is about giving to the most important resource any society has—our children.

This book was intended to be my gift to my children. I hope they find it valuable. I hope you will find it valuable, too.

— George S. Everly, Jr.
July, 2008

Contents

Lesson #3
Teach Your Children to Take Responsibility for Their Actions

Lesson #4
Making the Most Important Investment of a Lifetime:
Invest in Your Health

PART TWO
B = BELIEFS TO PROMOTE RESILIENCY

LESSON #5
Learn the Power of Optimism

Introduction
and Some Initial Thoughts
on Being a Successful Parent

A Parent's Reflection

I hope that I may have the wisdom,
the strength, and the compassion to be all
that my children need in a parent.
I hope that I can show unconditional love and support
without over-indulgence in worldly goods,
or setting inappropriate expectations
for the nature of the world
in which they live.
And when I am gone from this world,
I hope to be judged not by how much I made,
but by how much I gave;
Not by how many names I dropped,
but by how many people hear my name
and think fondly of me.
I hope my children will say of me:
"He was wise, he was silly, and with all of his flaws,
he was still a good man.
He was there for us. He taught us the value
of honesty, fidelity, family, and friends,
but above all else, he loved us.
He was there when we needed him,
and he will be with us always."

— GEORGE S. EVERLY, JR., PH.D.

Did you know that research has proven that if you get in the habit of writing down your thoughts and feelings during highly stressful times in your life, you can actually lower the stress you experience and gain greater insight into the things that plague you? I wrote "A Parent's Reflection" as I struggled to understand how I could be a better father, and perhaps even a better person. Fortunately, the people closest to me taught me that one of the most important challenges on earth—that of being a parent—is best fulfilled by building a foundation consisting of two simple actions: *presence* and *unconditional love.* When a friend and colleague asked me what I meant by *unconditional* love, I realized that the answer must come from the heart, not the brain, and that the answer will be different for all of us. I realized that the answer must be felt, not understood. Finally, I realized that for those who have felt unconditional love, no explanation is necessary; for those who have not, no explanation may ever be adequate.

As my eldest daughter and I sat on a hospital floor, helplessly waiting for her mother to take her last breath, those words echoed in my head. My life was changed by her passing. My priorities changed, and I realized that failure as a parent was not an option. There was simply too much at stake. I also realized that, if necessary, parents must be willing to sacrifice their today for their children's tomorrows. I later learned that I would willingly give up my preconceived notion of what my future would be, as well.

That same daughter subsequently married, and it was one of the happiest days of my life. At the rehearsal dinner, she gave me a gift that would warm any father's heart. It was a picture of her at about 2 years of age, eating an ice cream cone, although most of the ice cream was actually on her face. The inscription said, "Always Daddy's Little Girl." An additional inscription read, "All I am today I am because of you."

Although these words would be a tonic to any parent's soul, I knew that who she is today and what she has achieved are the result of many people—mostly her mother, if I am to be honest—and many other forces. I wanted to better understand what those forces were. This book describes one parent's journey of discovery, if not revelation. I wish I could say it was a journey based upon education and insight, because even though this is true to some degree, I made just about every mistake imaginable—so, a warning to the reader—beware the zeal of the newly reformed. Just kidding!

A LITTLE BACKGROUND

I guess I should start by telling you a little about myself, just to frame what I will say later in this book. I grew up in Catonsville, Maryland, a small town southwest of Baltimore. Through the guidance of a dedicated visionary, Mayor William Donald Schaefer, Baltimore was a city in transition. The established port and the steel mills were the backbone of the economy, but we all knew Baltimore was undergoing a renaissance that would yield great opportunities. My father believed this, and he convinced me of it, too. He was very optimistic.

My father parented by example. He took me shopping, taught me the basics of accounting and finance, and we went to church every Sunday. He was a self-reliant, reliable, child of the Great Depression. Raised on a farm, he studied schoolwork by lantern and often traveled by horse and buggy. He started working away from the farm at age 11.

After high school graduation, my father joined the army and was sent to Europe during World War II. He landed on Omaha Beach during the D-Day Campaign. After the war, he worked two jobs. He was honest, loyal, and true to his word. He never missed a day of work, and his two jobs never kept him from being a good dad. He was always there when I needed him. At my father's retirement party, one of his co-workers told me that in the 30 years he'd known my dad, he'd never heard an unkind word said about him. I have to believe the term *The Greatest Generation* was coined with my father in mind.

My mother was a stay-at-home mom. A twin, she was born and raised in the Deep South. I have very fond memories of visiting my relatives in Birmingham, Alabama, and the small town of Manchester, Georgia, each summer. Life seemed much simpler there. Although illness took my mother away from me at a relatively early age, I remember her energy, happiness, and love of life, but most importantly, the unconditional love she showed me.

The lifelong message given to me by both of my parents was their example of *reliability, fidelity,* and *commitment*—not just to each other, but to their son, as well. These concepts are easily translated into basic five principles:

1. If you give your word, you follow through. Promises do not have expiration dates.
2. Honesty is not the exception, it's the rule.
3. Employment is a career, not just a job. An income is something you *earn*, not something you are *owed*.
4. Take responsibility for your actions.
5. Your actions affect others, *always*. Therefore, always think about the consequences of your actions.

A story my father shared with me on the day I received my Ph.D. emphasizes his support and optimism: When I was in tenth grade, I was considered quite the underachiever, and my Dad was summoned to my high school one evening for a rather ominous meeting with my counselor. The counselor tried to persuade my father to remove me from high school and send me to trade school. "George will never get into college, and if he does, he'll never graduate," he said.

My father thanked the counselor for his concern and his guidance, but reassured him that my academic future was brighter than it might seem. In retrospect, I think it was my parents' belief in me and their constant encouragement that helped me overcome crippling dyslexia and what would later become known as *Attention Deficit Disorder* (ADD).

As far as I was concerned, I had a fantastic childhood—a *Leave It to Beaver* childhood (if this reference confuses you, watch the television re-runs). I was involved in organized athletics as a kid, but I was only an adequate athlete at best. In fact, I got my one and only athletic award at age 16—a patch showing I had made the baseball "All Stars" in my community. For me, that little felt patch stood for 4 years of hard work. I still have it on my desk.

TIMES HAVE CHANGED

Every time I walk into my youngest daughter's room, I am struck by all of the trophies she has received just for participating in swimming, soccer, and lacrosse. Basically, they are prizes for "showing up." Of course, I'm happy if they help her self-esteem. But, I worry about the expectations these trophies might set for later life. Will she learn that she deserves to be rewarded simply because of her presence, rather than her performance? Will she grow up with a sense of entitlement that sets the stage for bitterness and disappointment in later life—when someone finally holds her accountable for how she performs, not just for "showing up?

How can I best prepare my kids for a world that does not love them as much as I do—a world that might not recognize their inner strengths or their unique beauty and intrinsic value?

PARENTS AS TEACHERS

Who can be more woven into your life than your parents? How do we, as parents, weave strong, productive, and happy lives for our children, lives that are constructed with good resilient fiber? I've traveled the world—thirty-two countries on six continents—from the frozen North to the sweltering subtropics, from refugee camps to palaces, from villages without running water or electricity to the most energetic and sophisticated cities in the world. During all of my travels, I've tried to learn what makes people successful, and how parents can help their children become successful, resilient, and happy.

> *What you leave behind is not what is engraved in stone monuments, but what is woven into the lives of others.*
> —ATHENIAN PHILOSOPHER PERICLES (CA. 495–429 BC)

Every year, books are written about how to get what you want out of life—whether this means money, cars, education, or the perfect spouse. This book, on the other hand, is not about getting, it's about *giving*.

Of the many noble professions, teaching might be the most noble of all. Teachers enter the lives of children at the most formative and critical times, and provide knowledge, direction, and support that can help children grow, prosper, and realize their potentials, no matter what this might mean. Did you ever consider that, as a parent, you are your child's first teacher? Well, you are. And the home is your child's first classroom. If you think about it, parenting is also somewhat like coaching. A successful coach motivates athletes to achieve their best performance. Similarly, successful parents motivate their children to realize their full potential. Research on coaching and performance has found that the best motivators of young people appear to be:

1. The need to belong to a desired group (a need for affiliation).
2. The desire to be good at something (the need to excel).

Do these sound familiar? Oh, and there is something else.

3. The ability to control stress so as to avoid getting "stressed out," "psyched out," or "burned out," is also a necessary skill that affects motivation. How many promising careers in academics, athletics, or even the performing arts were never realized because the person could not handle the associated stress and pressure? I've lived long enough now to see many promising careers end in frustration because of a lack of psychological resilience. How many challenges were never undertaken because of the fear of failure? (I need only look at my own life to see a few of those.) Well, this book challenges you to be the teacher and coach your children need; maybe even the teacher and coach some of us wish we would have had growing up.

THE A-B-Cs OF RESILIENCY
So, what are the keys to successful parenting and childhood development?

Although I knew that different children need different styles of parenting in order to help them become happy and successful, I was sure there are also plenty of common needs that all children share. So, I wondered if there were certain essential needs that—if satisfied—would define successful parenting? If so, what are those essential needs?

The well-known psychologist Dr. Abraham Maslow believed that until the *basic* needs, such as the physical needs for food, shelter, and clothing, were met, it was impossible to fulfill the more advanced needs of human development. *Advanced needs* include the ability to care for others, the ability to think well of yourself, and achieving self-esteem. However, many children live in situations in which their basic physical needs are often neglected—yet these children grow and prosper. They learn to appreciate and care for others, just as they learn to care for themselves.

Some people might say that the need to feel safe is an essential one, and, of course, feeling safe is important to healthy development. But, certainly, there are many instances in which children have felt unsafe as they grew up. Yet these children did well and had satisfying lives. Some even learned to feel safe.

All kids need love from their parents. This is the foundation for other aspects of parenting. But we have all known folks (maybe even ourselves) who grew up without unconditional love, but somehow learned to love others.

What else is needed beyond the physical needs and the need to be safe and loved? Is there something even more essential?

Other than what has just been mentioned, I believe the most essential lesson parents can teach their children is the ability to cope with stress and adversity. This is known as *resilience*, which can be thought of as the ability to be *resistant* to stress (a kind of immunity), as well as the ability to *rebound* from adversity. It also may be the critical difference between happiness or regret, success or failure. Wouldn't it be great if we could learn this in school?

In addition to taking care of basic physical needs, safety, and love, I believe all parents have an obligation to help their children become stress-resilient. This should not be confused with protecting children from all adversity, however. *Adversity happens*—to paraphrase a popular bumper sticker! There will come a time when your child will encounter adversity when he isn't with you. The irony is that you'll know you've been successful in your job as a parent and teacher because your child won't need you in stressful situations as he once did. He will be able to handle adversity alone. If you want to be a successful parent, strive to make your role obsolete. Strive to raise your children to be happy, healthy, and productive—with you when possible, without you when necessary.

How do we do this? We must teach children to develop the *inner strength* that makes all things possible. Inner strength is as simple as "A-B-C," but, in this case, A-B-C stands for a powerful set of **A**CTIONS, **B**ELIEFS, and **C**ODES that form the core strength of personal character. They amount to seven "lessons to be learned." Think of them as the A-B-Cs of the stress-proofing and resiliency lessons you will teach your kids.

The premise of this book is simple: Resiliency and stress management are not only health-promoting skills for life; they are the essential keys to finding happiness. As such, they should be taught to children and teenagers as soon as they are capable of understanding the concepts. Unlike many books on resiliency and stress management, this book does not teach techniques, per se—it teaches seven pillars upon which a stress-resilient life and the pursuit of happiness can be built. The collective wisdom in this simple book should be essential reading for all parents and teachers of children and young adults.

The Resilient Child contains seven teaching tools called *The Seven Essential Lessons for a Resilient Child.* These lessons are divided into three parts:

- Actions: Lessons 1–4
- Beliefs: Lessons 5–6
- Codes: Lesson 7

Our journey begins with **ACTIONS.** The four actions discussed in Part One are essential to building true inner strength, resiliency, and happiness:

Lesson #1: Friendship and Support. Develop strong relationships with friends and mentors.

Lesson #2: Courage. Learn to make difficult decisions.

Lesson #3: Responsibility. Own your actions. (This might be
shocking, we know!)

Lesson #4: Self-investment. The best way to help others, and
yourself, is to stay healthy.

Part Two is about **BELIEFS**. These are judgments, expectations, or a form of acceptance. Our actions need support from our
beliefs. "As you think, so shall you be." That's where optimism
comes into play:

Lesson #5: Optimism. Learn to think on the bright side and
use the power of the self-fulfilling prophecy.

Lesson #6: Faith. Believe in something greater than yourself

Part Three is about the **CODE.** A *code* is an overarching set
of principles or rules that ultimately serves to guide all of a person's actions:

Lesson #7. Learn to follow a moral compass and strive to have
integrity

I believe these seven essential lessons can help children develop
the inner strength of character needed to enhance resiliency in facing
the challenges of life. As parents, it's your job to teach, coach, protect,
and love your children. We hope the lessons in this book will help
provide a parental counterbalance to the stress that all children
ultimately encounter. It's designed to help you teach your children
how to avoid stress, how to avoid the excesses and distortions that

bombard us today, and how to be resilient, regardless of the events they encounter in their lives. We hope this foundation will serve them for the rest of their lives, giving them a better chance of success in marriage and career, and helping them avoid many emotional pitfalls.

The essential actions, beliefs, and codes that shape true resiliency in the face of distress and adversity can prevent debilitating stress, if learned early enough. Think of this as an *acquired immunity* to the distress that robs people of their health, steals their happiness, ruins their marriages, and stifles their careers.

This book discusses research and what I have learned from working with people under stress, but it also tells stories. Most of these stories reflect the experiences that I have had as a scientist, psychologist, teacher, husband, father, and friend. Although I have modified actual incidents, and some of the stories have been integrated to emphasize a point—and so that the individuals involved will remain anonymous—the basic elements represent actual experiences. We've added "HomeWork" sections to help you think about the material in the book, and to help both you and your children practice the lessons we discuss. At the end of each lesson, you will find a list of questions you can ask yourself and your children to help you focus on the material and understand the concepts in the lesson. Also included are suggested conversations you can have with your children to reinforce learning.

My basic premise in this book is that we must focus on protecting our most precious resource—our children! I've written for years about how adults can better manage the stress in their lives, and my clinical practice has been based on helping adults recover from physical and mental illnesses caused by excessive stress. It finally occurred to me that if these adults had been taught to manage stress early in life, they would never have needed to be clinically treated later.

We must teach our children not just how to react in moments of distress, but how to prevent it in the first place. We must also teach our children to live their lives in a way that gives them fond memories, not regret—lives of pride and happiness, not ones full of excuses and despair. This book was created to be my gift to my own children—but I hope you will find it worthy of being a gift for your children, too.

Part One:

ACTIONS TO
PROMOTE RESILIENCY

*Actions may be thought of
as the manner in which you behave
toward others and toward yourself.*

The Value of Friends, Mentors, and the Support of Others

I HAVE BEEN FORTUNATE IN MY LIFE to have had many acquaintances and a blessed cadre of true friends. I was not always sure of the difference. One night, when I was 20 years old, I began to learn the difference. The lesson would be strengthened throughout my life, and it's a lesson that all parents need to teach their children.

THE NATURE OF FRIENDSHIP

I was living at college and had just gotten a new roommate. I had known him since primary school, but we had really never been close. I was fortunate enough to have a car, but he didn't. One night, he called me around midnight and asked me to pick him up at one of the dorms on campus. I was in bed trying to get some sleep, so my initial response was "Are you kidding?" He seemed to be as perplexed by my response as I was by his request. Clearly, we were working from two different sets of assumptions. He expected I would help him when he needed a ride, no matter what the circumstances.

You have not lived today until you have done something for someone who can never repay you.
– JOHN BUNYON

When I realized there was more involved in his request than just a needing a ride, I put my clothes on and went to pick him up. We never spoke of it again, but that night changed my life forever. Ahh, how the little things in life can have such a big impact. I had finally gained some insight into what friendship was about. You see, I was an only child, and he was one of five children. This experience gave me some valuable insight into the difference between growing up *independently* versus *interdependently*—being connected to other people. Sometimes you need to go out of your way to help others because that's just what friends do.

A GOOD MAN AND THE GIFT PRINCIPLE

Years later, my notion of friendship was still continuing to evolve. My life unfolded in a manner I could not have predicted. Professionally, I had authored several well-regarded textbooks on treating stress-related disease. But, my true talent was diagnostic assessment. I was able to quickly and effectively identify the most prominent aspects of a disorder and treat it efficiently.

I was asked on one occasion to see a man who was exhibiting signs of neurologic dysfunction. He was only 41 years old, and his primary-care physician had assumed his problems were stress-related. I decided to visit the man at his office, an environment in which he would feel comfortable. He was a successful businessman and had recently purchased the company for which he had once worked. An economic downturn was causing a significant amount of increased stress for him and his family. In addition to his neurologic complaints, he had significantly elevated blood pressure.

My task was to perform a type of initial assessment that could be thought of as a "mental status examination." The goal of such an exam is to challenge each major neuropsychological system in order to assess its ability to function. The key is to make this assessment feel more like a conversation than a clinical procedure.

I liked this man instantly. He seemed hard-working, optimistic, compassionate, and intelligent, and he had strong family values and strong religious faith. And I later learned how kind and accepting he was. As our conversation progressed, I observed that he had an array of problems unlike anything I had ever seen at one time, but that I had read about. My prognosis for him was poor, and I immediately referred him to a neurologist. I was saddened by what I had seen, and hoped that I was wrong in my initial impressions. Unfortunately, I was not. He died 9 months later from a rare and aggressive degenerative disease.

Before I left his office, he said something to me that I remember with great gratitude. I call it "The Gift Principle." We talked about gifts during our conversation, and he said to me, making a scriptural reference, "The only true gift is the gift you cannot afford to give." As if he knew he was seriously ill, he said he wanted to make sure his family and his employees were taken care of and that the company, upon which many people depended, would continue.

I see his warm smile and think of his words every time a friend asks me for a favor, or when I am asked to donate to a worthy cause. But, perhaps more importantly, I hear his words whenever I think of the true meaning of friendship. As another friend once told me, friendship is not real until it is tested.

I attended the funeral of that 41-year-old man, and I was struck by how many people's lives he had touched in a positive but unassuming way. I was touched by the obvious love and caring for him and his family, and how connected they were to their many friends and the community. It was obvious that he was a *good* man, and that he would be missed.

Can we aspire to be anything more than a good person and leave a legacy of kindness and support for others, especially our loved ones? I still think of him fondly, and I am thankful that he was part of my life, albeit far too briefly. I am grateful for his wisdom and for the gift he gave me. I often wonder what he would say about the manner in which his company and his children have fared. His children are all grown. I hope they know what an extraordinary man their father was. His wisdom is worthy of being passed on to our children, as well. What do you think?

Blessed is he who is surrounded by those of a good heart and an unwavering supportive presence… I am truly blessed.

BEING PRESENT

Remember my roommate and friend from college? Well, fast-forward 30 years. Our friendship grew, and many of our interests stayed the same. He was the godfather of my oldest daughter and, although events came between us, our friendship remained strong. He became a very successful businessman. Although we had been competitive when we were growing up, I can honestly say that I rejoiced in his successes. He is a man of honesty and devotion, who deserves success. He even became a bit of a business mentor for me.

I received a phone call from him on an unseasonably warm fall day, a Sunday. He said he was in Philadelphia and was coming home on the train. I thought the call unusual because he never called me on a Sunday. He said he was bringing his youngest daughter home from college. She was a beautiful and gifted young lady, who had been having problems adjusting to college life as a first-semester freshman. I quickly said that I thought bringing her home for a respite was a good idea. "Give her a semester off, and then let her resume," I said.

He interrupted me and said, "No, you don't understand—I'm bringing her home to bury her."

I was speechless. I had spent most of my professional life learning to help people in their greatest moments of need, but now I felt helpless at a time when my friend was in need. He gave me a brief description of the events that had led up to the phone call and, as soon as I hung up the phone, I grabbed my jacket and began driving to meet him at the train station.

From the car, I called my oldest daughter at college and told her the tragic news. I must admit, the main reason I called was just to make sure that she was okay. At one point she said, "Daddy, what are you going to do when you get there?" I said I wasn't sure. But she pushed the issue. Finally, I told her that I was just going to show up and *be present*—because that's what friends do for each other. My friends in the chaplaincy even have a term for it: They call it *the ministry of presence*.

When I reached the train station, my friend, his wife, and his other children were just exiting the building. I was unsure of what to say, other than "I'm so sorry." I hugged them all, because sometimes touch can say more than words. I grabbed their bags and carried them to their car. I followed them to the funeral home, where they did what no parents should ever have to do: pick out a casket for their child.

I waited for about 2 hours, and then we drove to their home, where friends and family were gathering to offer condolences. I sat in their kitchen for several hours feeling useless. Finally, I left without saying good-bye.

A handwritten note from my friend was delivered in Tuesday's mail. It said simply,

Dear Pal,
Thanks for all you did for me on Sunday.
I will NEVER, EVER forget it.

With all that he had to do, and with all that was on his mind, he took the time to send me a note. Some months later, I saw his oldest daughter, who said, "Thanks for all you did for my father the day we brought my sister home." All I had done was show up and be there for them.

That's what mothers and fathers do for their children. They show up and watch the school play, the baseball game, and the spelling bee. When they can't be there in person, they call, leave notes, or show their love in other ways. My wife used to pack a lunch for my oldest daughter and slip a little note inside that said, "Have a great day! Love, Mommy."

Some years after my friend lost his daughter, my world and that of my family was once again turned upside down. Each year, my friend and I would get together to celebrate our respective birthdays. Every year, we would find a card that makes fun of the aging process. This year, the card I received was different:

George, I'm ALWAYS wishing the best for you—you deserve it! Just remember, even though you've gone through some tough times lately, there are people who care for you and will be there for you, too.

Tears came to my eyes as I read his card and remembered the power of friendship. I also thought about the 41-year-old man who had touched so many lives in a positive way.

So, what are the take-away messages for parents and for our kids?

As parents, show up. Be there for your children…be present, if not in body then in mind. Reach out to them any way you can. Never let their hesitation to accept your help deter you from offering. They will remember your offers for the rest of their lives.

Encourage your children to make friends, to establish networks, to stay in touch even when distance or circumstances make personal contact difficult. Teach them that friendship is more about giving than receiving. Friendship is about being present.

FRIENDS VERSUS ACQUAINTANCES

Friendship is a term that has come to mean a close personal relationship. It's more than acquaintanceship. An acquaintance is someone you know and who knows you. Acquaintanceship is based upon mutual knowledge of one another. Friendship is far more. Friendship is based upon mutual trust, esteem, and, if necessary, an unhesitating willingness to offer support without any expectation that you will be repaid. Friendships are built on honesty. You probably have many acquaintances, but far fewer real friends. Your children should be encouraged to avoid confusing acquaintances with friends because it can lead to disappointment.

> *To the soul, there is hardly anything more healing than friendship.*
> –THOMAS MOORE

Friends are truly happy for your success, and they will act with courage on your behalf. I have many true friends, but three are the closest. One man and his wife have been by my side throughout much of my life. He encouraged me to join his private practice and opened doors for me that I would not have otherwise known existed. They both encouraged me, if not promoted me, at the high points in my life. When the inevitable difficulties came along, they were there to support me, to advocate, and defend.

Their most endearing quality is their courage to do what they believe is right, even if it's unpopular. Friends do not stand by and passively accept injustices when they are done to other friends. Teach your children that friendship means being willing to stand up and offer support even when it requires courage.

A long habit of not thinking a thing wrong gives it a superficial appearance of being right.
–THOMAS PAINE

The failure to speak out against a wrong endorses it as being right and serves to further injure those who have already been hurt. Teach your children that, when they find people willing to stand up for what's right, they must cherish them because they are capable of being true friends.

THE VALUE OF FRIENDSHIP

How can we know the value of friendship? In his book *Preventive Psychiatry*, Gerald Caplan wrote that a psychological crisis was a response to a stressful or traumatic event in which your psychological defenses are overwhelmed and your usual coping mechanisms fail. In such situations, we are challenged beyond our ability to cope, and it is usually prudent to seek support from others. Research has consistently shown that the support of family, friends, and co-workers is the single most effective means of enhancing resilience in stressful situations.

Support from others can help a person overcome even the most difficult problems. When you recruit the assistance of friends in virtually any endeavor, you will have enlisted new perspectives on an issue that might be too close for you to see

Friendship makes prosperity more shining and lessens adversity by dividing and sharing it.
–CICERO

objectively or creatively. Friends have a way of underscoring, even amplifying your victories. They can diffuse the angst of defeat. Joseph Addison noted, "Friendship improves happiness and abates misery by doubling our joys and dividing our grief."

Early in my career, I had the privilege of meeting Stewart Wolf, one of the founding fathers of the field of psychosomatic medicine. I had read his work for years, and it was truly seminal research into the effects of psychological and social factors on physical health. His book *The Power of Clan: The Influences of Human Relationships on Heart Disease* summarized some of his ground-breaking research.

The book told the story of Roseto, Pennsylvania, and Dr. Wolf's 25-year investigation of the health of it inhabitants. Roseto was a "medical marvel" because, although its inhabitants possessed significant risk factors for heart disease, such as smoking, high-cholesterol diets, and a sedentary lifestyle, the inhabitants appeared to be relatively immune to heart disease. The death rate in Roseto from heart disease was less than half that of surrounding towns.

Our first impression of Roseto in 1962 was of an extremely clean, neat, well-kept town. The townspeople still clung to their hierarchical family structure, and they felt a need to protect themselves against community gossip by admonishing their children to avoid offending others.

–STEWARD WOLF, M.D

Dr. Wolf's research team endeavored to discover the secret of health that seemed to grace the community. He discovered that the protective factor was not in the water or the air, but rather in the people themselves. Their social cohesiveness, traditional family values, a family-oriented social structure in which three and even four generations resided in the same household, and emotional support had resulted in immunity from heart disease.

The mutually protective social network of Roseto also shared an established standard of values and behavior. Unfortunately, over time, its residents slowly abandoned their family-oriented social structure, and the prevalence of heart disease increased accordingly, until it was the equivalent of the surrounding towns. The immunity that the social structure had afforded was lost.

A younger community member commented, "We are aggressive about getting another job to earn more money so we can be a two-car family." Another young adult commented, "I envy other people. I work hard so I can be proud of what I have, and I hope to be able to have more things. I worry about it."

As our children strive for their own identities and independence, we should encourage them not to abandon their ties to family and friends. We should teach them that interdependence with family and friends does not weaken them, but rather strengthens them. Efforts to stay connected will be among the best investments they can ever make.

MENTORS

Mentors are people who teach you, advise you, support you, and—when necessary—protect you, kind of like parents who aren't related to you.

I remember my first interview with Dr. David McClelland at Harvard University. He was to be my advisor, and he would become my mentor…and friend. It was a hot August day, but I was perspiring more from my anxiety about meeting one of the founding fathers of the field of behavioral medicine than I was from the 90-degree heat and the corduroy jacket I was wearing. Dr. McClelland was the first scientist to show that the potency of the immune system could be increased or decreased by the emotions a person experienced. This was an idea previously thought to be absurd, even by immunologists.

I had written several books by that time in my career. When Dr. McClelland had finished reviewing my resumé, he looked at me from behind his desk and said, "You've done well for yourself at your young age. In my experience, there is almost always someone who has served as a friend or mentor to provide motivation and assistance in careers such as yours. Who played that role in your life?"

Dr. McClelland was insightful, and in my case quite correct. The complete answer to his question is a subject for another time, but his comment that I couldn't have achieved what I had without the guidance and support of others was completely accurate.

Although Dr. McClelland would become a mentor, I had prospered from another mentor—in fact two of them. Dr. Daniel Girdano reignited the desire to learn. (Parents, can you imagine a more wonderful gift for your "student" than the hunger for knowledge?) And, there was Dr. Theodore Millon, who entered my life at a critical period, providing compassion and support on a personal level as well as immeasurable intellectual and academic stimulation.

Although not a mentor, I even thought about my first real "girlfriend" in high school. Go figure that one out (oh, that's right, that's *my* job). Nevertheless, Dr. McClelland's observation that our lives are built upon the presence, caring, and support of others (friendship, mentorship) is an important observation to keep in mind. So…

Teach your children to seek mentors…parental surrogates when necessary. I am often asked by students who want to apply for postgraduate education where they should go to school. My answer is, "Go wherever you can find a mentor, someone who will take a personal interest in your education and your success."

HomeWork

- Write the names of your two or three closest friends. Next to each name, explain why you chose that person for a friend. Describe a specific situation in which each person demonstrated his or her friendship.
- Ask your children to do this same exercise. After everyone has finished writing, talk about what you've written and what constitutes a close friend.

- Write the names of two people, other than your spouse, family, or parents, who have made significant and positive contributions to who you are and what you have achieved in your life, so far. After each name, write a brief description about their contributions—not just what they did, but how their actions helped shape you as a person.
- Ask your children to do this same exercise. After everyone has finished writing, talk about what you've written and how others contribute to your life.

BUILDING SOLID RELATIONSHIPS

The support of others is a precious commodity, especially in times of great need. Beyond family, such support often must be earned. Working hard to earn the friendship of others is an investment in your own future, as well as the future of others. Here are some thoughts on how you can teach your children to create a support network and build friendships, emphasizing that "to find a good friend, you must be a good friend":

- Friendship is based upon trust. Sometimes, you must first trust the other person before you can expect him to trust you.
- Friendship is based upon loyalty and fidelity. Promises don't have expirations dates.
- Friendship is based on kindness. Show genuine kindness to others. People will judge you by the manner in which you

treat others—and they will also treat you in the same way as you treat them.

- People will eventually hear whatever you say about them, so say kind things and be complimentary whenever you can.
- People who speak unkindly about others will speak unkindly of you.
- Friendship is based upon honoring others. One of the greatest gifts you can give another person is to honor her and help her feel *important.* Help her be a "star"; help her shine.
- Most importantly, friendship is based upon being of assistance when you are needed. Thus, friendship means assist-

One of the most important ways to manifest integrity is to be loyal to those who are not present. In doing so, we build the trust of those who are present.
–Stephen Covey

ing others in times of need and expecting *nothing* in return. Friendship means giving that which is difficult to give, and doing so without resentment or regret.

Early in my career, I was collaborating with a senior colleague to write a research grant. As we discussed previous research, I was particularly critical of other researchers. My colleague, who was an early mentor in other aspects of my life, brought an abrupt end to my comments. In a supportive but emphatic way, he simply said, "There are two types of people: Those who contribute and those who detract. You must learn that the best way to build your career is through your own achievements, not by attacking the achievements of others. People will always remember what type of person you are, and they will trust or distrust you accordingly."

Seldom have I heard words that were truer or more genuinely wise. People who have only

As far as possible, without surrender, be on good terms with all persons.
–Max Ehrmann

negatives to offer are soon forgotten—those who contribute in a constructive way become part of history.

Teach your children that, in order to win friends, they must *be* a friend—supportive and kind. Never ridicule or devalue others. By doing so your children will become trusted confidantes and part of their friends' "trusted inner circle."

PICK YOUR FRIENDS AND MENTORS CAREFULLY: THE TWO BEST QUESTIONS YOU CAN ASK ABOUT ANOTHER PERSON

Teach your children to pick their friends and acquaintances carefully. Betrayal is a pain that lasts a lifetime. People who are unfaithful to others will eventually be unfaithful to you. Those who betray others will betray you. So, be picky, picky, picky when choosing your friends! Consistency of behavior can be a clue in picking reliable friends.

Exercise caution... for the world is full of trickery.
–MAX EHRMANN

As a psychologist, I have been trained in the diagnostic assessment of people and their behavior. This often means that I have to assess a person's integrity, honesty, and trustworthiness as part of a job application or security clearance. I've spent thousands of hours refining my skills, but the most powerful tool I ever learned was taught to me in a 5-minute conversation.

Psychological tests are certainly important, but never forget that there is nothing more powerful than the well-phrased question.
–HENRY MURRAY, M.D.

Dr. Henry Murray was a biochemist and physician who founded the Boston Psychoanalytic Society. His comment on psychological tests helped me put them in perspective. He chaired the Harvard Psychological Clinic and developed *The Thematic Apperception Test,* one of the most widely used psychological tests in the world.

Let me share with you the most revealing questions I've learned. If someone does something that is inappropriate, immoral, unethical, or just plain wrong, rather than immediately offering an excuse for them, simply ask yourself these questions:

1. *"Has he ever done this before?"* The answer to this question will help you distinguish an honest mistake from an enduring pattern of behavior. Everyone makes mistakes. A mistake is what you did. Repeating the same behavior is no longer a "mistake," it's who you are. More on this later.

2. *"What type of person behaves like that?"* In other words: *"What type of person does what that person just did?"* The answer to this question gets to the core issue of whether this is the type of person you want as a friend, acquaintance, business partner, or even as a spouse!

The answers to these questions can tell you more about another person than any battery of psychological tests. The best thing about these two questions is that children can learn them and understand the concepts behind them.

HomeWork

- Ask yourself those two questions about a few people you have recently met or do not know very well. See what insight you get about those individuals.
- In order to deepen your child's understanding, when you see inappropriate behavior or hear your children describe

behavior on the part of their friends that is either positive or questionable, pause and ask your child, "Gee, what kind of person would do that?"

- Past behavior predicts future behavior, but not completely. If you are inclined to trust someone who has acted in a less than trustworthy or honorable manner in the past, ask yourself, "What has changed about this person? Why is he (or she) more likely to act responsibly and honorably now than in the past?" People are, indeed, capable of remarkable changes, but there is always a reason for why they changed. Prompt your kids to ask the same question.

WARNING: AVOID TOXIC PEOPLE!

Teach your children that one of the best ways to develop great friendships is to make friends with positive people who have integrity. But most importantly, they should *learn to avoid toxic people*. How many times did your parents tell you that you are judged by the company you keep—and that they worried about you hanging around with the wrong people because they would hurt you or get you into trouble? Just as the environment has its toxins, humanity includes toxic people. Recognizing and avoiding toxic people is an essential skill that all children need to learn as early in life as possible.

Tips for making good choices in friendships:

- Some people put on a facade to fool you into believing that's who they really are. But, until you understand a person's true personality—which is based on a consistent pattern of thoughts, feelings, and behaviors—you won't understand that person at a deeper level.

- You can't truly know someone until you see them under stress. People can fake being charming, honest, and trustworthy for extended periods of time under low-stress conditions. But, the real person usually emerges when they are challenged or under stress.
- The best predictor of future behavior is past behavior, and the best predictor of consistent future behavior is the consistent behavior of the past.

Toxic people spread unhappiness and personal suffering. They ultimately poison everything they come in touch with: other people, careers, businesses, marriages, and especially children. These people are virtually immune to insight, remorse, or lasting positive change. I'm not talking about people with criminal personalities, but rather people who live and work with us every day.

There are at least four basic types of toxic people: the seductive, overly dramatic person; the aggressive-selfish person; the negative, complaining person; and people with Type A behavior patterns. Let's take a closer look and see if you can recognize any of these folks in your daily life.

The Seductive, Overly Dramatic Person

The seductive, overly dramatic person can be great fun. Often the life of the party, they are usually physically attractive, charming, and exciting. They do things to attract attention, which might include sexually flirtatious, seductive actions and dress. They are often *risk-takers*.

This might sound great, at first, but reality soon sets in. Some of these individuals are painfully insecure, and this pattern of behavior is actually a way of compensating for their insecurity. These people are usually quite superficial. They judge themselves and others by external criteria, such as what they have, how they look, and who they know. They often use sexuality as a type of *currency* to get what they want—and it often works, at least for a while. The problem is that this way of acting, which is caused by a deep sense of insecurity, worsens with age. Unfortunately, the classic mid-life crisis is inevitable, as their sexuality lessens in value. When the crisis does come, it's massive: infidelity, repetitive plastic surgery, abandonment of their children and previous friends, and changing or abandoning their career. The rationale for such dramatic change is that these things were "holding them back."

Making a dramatic lifestyle shift provides greater time to engage in desperate attempts to recapture former youth, beauty, and/or athletic prowess. It can be consuming and self-defeating. The craving for attention, as a remedy for insecurity, becomes obsessional and self-destructive, but not until they have consumed and discarded the people around them. In an attempt to find a partner who will compensate for their weaknesses, they often inadvertently select partners who are controlling, selfish, and abusive, or at least manipulative. This type of story does not have a happy ending.

The Aggressive-Selfish Person

Aggressive and selfish individuals, most often males, tend to be adventurous and risk-taking. They are superficially charming, glib, and exciting. Inclined to be possessive, verbally abusive, and sometimes even physically abusive, they tend to be controlling and intimidating toward other people. They seek out friends and partners of the opposite sex who tend to be needy and look up to them. They tend to see themselves as assertive, rather than aggressive. They have a sense of entitlement that leads to a remarkable selfishness. As a result, their entitled selfishness extends to usurping the rights of others as if it was their God-given prerogative. Rules, and even laws, are acceptable only if they do not keep them from doing something they want to do; otherwise, such rules and laws are seen as not being applicable to them.

Many teenage girls, as well as people who have low self-esteem, are often targeted by, and sometimes even attracted to, these types of people because they see them as protectors. The protection soon wanes, and verbal and physical abuse often follows.

Ironically, as arrogant and self-centered as these individuals appear to be, their behavior usually masks their own deep sense of insecurity for which they spend a lifetime trying to compensate. It is not uncommon to see these individuals collect things, even people they can show off, as examples of their success. So-called "trophy wives," exotic cars, large homes, yachts, and expensive jewelry can all be part of this person's collection, which is designed to convince themselves that they are worthy. The problem is that the quest to compensate for their insecurity never ends. They use people and things, and then discard them in a never-ending cycle of compensation. They do not recognize interpersonal boundaries, because they consider everything to be theirs for the taking. They are prone to midlife crises, tend to have multiple affairs and marriages, and they get angrier as they get older. If they have children, they often develop conflicts with them as the children age and their parental control over them lessens. The children ultimately recognize these parents as controlling and distance themselves. These parents then see their children as ungrateful.

The Negative, Complaining Person

The negative, complaining person never seems really happy. Nothing is ever good enough for them (that's the negative part), and they are more than willing to let you know about it (that's the complaining part). They appear pleasant on a superficial level, but the longer you know them, the more erratic their behavior becomes, and it is often interspersed with an obstinate or manipulative quality. They have mastered the use of passive-aggressive behavior as a means of making everyone else as unhappy as they are ("misery loves company"). Passive-aggressive behavior is aggression that is masked so as to avoid retaliation. For example, a person might say, "Gee, I really like your new dress. That style was popular 5 to 10 years ago, wasn't it?" Even though the negative person has insulted someone with a new dress by suggesting it is out of style, if challenged she can always say, "But, I said I really liked it." In general, these people are cynical and pessimistic.

These people are actually dangerous. By this I mean that they have a tendency to be very self-defeating by doing things that get themselves and others (your children!) into trouble. These folks are very controlling, but they never learned how to do it. They were usually raised in households where one or both parents were critical, controlling individuals. As a result, people with this type of personality never really learned how to take charge of their own lives in a constructive way, so they take charge in self-defeating, passive-aggressive, manipulative ways. The major reason that they are so dangerous is that they self-destruct their marriages, careers, and interpersonal relationships. Our children need to learn to recognize and avoid these folks at all costs, lest they become caught in the self-destructive "explosion."

Type A Behavior

The last person on our "avoid at all costs" list is the Type A. Sounds good, doesn't it? Wrong! In the mid-1970s, two Stanford cardiologists, Ray Rosenman and Myer Friedman, wrote the book *Type A Behavior and Your Heart.* They discussed years of research documenting the fact that a certain behavior pattern, or personality type, could dramatically increase the risk of coronary heart disease. They called this pattern *Type A.*

The Type A pattern consisted of a classic "workaholic" syndrome. Read this list carefully, because you might work for one of these folks one day. Type A individuals are:

- Chronically in a rush, even if there is no objective reason to be in a rush. They are in a chronic state of time urgency as they rush around, often to end up waiting. They hate crowds, lines, and people who speak slowly. They will even finish sentences for people who speak too slowly.
- Always doing more than one thing at a time.
- Competitive—very competitive. They have to make a win–lose situation out of everything. The might bend the rules in order to win, even cheat. They are very poor losers, and they are often quite hostile toward others.
- Impulsive. Type A individuals hate to wait and are eager to act. They will act often without thinking or planning. Seldom do Type A individuals take the time to read directions.

Research tried to identify which of these factors was the most toxic. Finally, evidence suggested that chronic hostility was the most lethal. The hostility appeared to emerge from a deep sense of insecurity, and the "win at all costs" attitude of the Type A was an attempt to compensate for it.

Type A people are often initially attractive to others. They are smart, driven, often exciting, and assumed to be successful in the future. As a result, they usually have little difficulty attracting dating partners. But, early in the relationship, or marriage, it becomes clear that their highest priority is their own success, not their partner. So, it is not uncommon to see relationships strained and their partners becoming frustrated, unless of course the Type A person "outgrows" the pattern.

So, what have we learned about toxic people?

- Teach your children to AVOID THEM whenever possible.
- Teach your children to protect themselves if they have to be around such people by trying NEVER to rely on them.
- The characteristics that seem to make them so toxic are also the characteristics that can be attractive at first, such as risk-taking, confidence, aggressiveness, and seductiveness. They mask other more toxic qualities, such as arrogance, selfishness, a sense of entitlement, persistent, underlying anger, impulsiveness, and insecurity.
- In many cases, their toxic nature appears to come from the last factor listed above: a deep sense of insecurity that stems from interactions with their parents. So, we come full circle. Parents, are you listening?

THE MOST IMPORTANT QUESTION OF ALL

So, what is the essential lesson to be learned about picking people as potential friends and more?

My oldest daughter came to me a decade ago after a series of tumultuous relationships with boys. She seemed frustrated that she hadn't found that "someone special." She asked, "Daddy, how will I ever know I've found the right guy?"

I had not rehearsed the answer to this question, but did you ever notice that sometimes your mouth opens and the right words come out? Often, it's just the opposite. But, in this case, without thinking or hesitating, I simply said, "You will know you've met the right guy when he believes and acts as if he has been truly blessed to have you in his life—and at the same time, you'll feel truly blessed to have him in yours."

DEALING WITH GRIEF

As parents, we have an obligation to prepare our children for the inevitability of loss of friends and loved ones, and the grief that might be associated with it. Grief can be thought of as the sadness associated with loss. Most commonly, we associate grief with the loss of another person, but we can grieve for other things as well.

We might grieve the loss of a pet or friend, or the loss of a role; for example, our role as a mother or father when the children grow up and leave home. We might grieve the loss of our role as an employee when we retire; athletes sometimes mourn the loss of their abilities with aging. A husband or wife will grieve over a divorce or separation.

Resilience in the face of loss is made easier by making sure there is no unfinished business between us and the person or situation we have lost. This can be easily achieved when the loss is antici-pated, such as in retirement, children moving out on their own, and terminal illness. But, even in situations where the loss is not anticipated, there are things we can teach children that can reduce the pain of grief.

- First, help your children focus on the positive aspects of the relationship, and the things they gained from the relation-ship, not what they lost because the relationship is gone.
- Second, try to focus on the enduring positive aspects that are left behind, such as experiences that were gained and lessons learned.
- Third, do not focus on how the children can live without the lost person or thing. Rather, help them focus on how to live in the warmth of the memories and lessons learned as a result of the person or thing being a part of their lives, no matter how brief.

HomeWork

- Help your children practice *empathy*, which can be explained as trying to think like someone else thinks or feel what someone else feels. It's a role reversal in which you try to be the other person for a few moments. Empathy is very helpful in defusing arguments. So, before getting angry or frustrated with another person, have your children ask themselves:
  - "Gee, I wonder how that person is feeling right now?"
  - "I wonder what's making them feel that way?"
- Encourage your children to be helpful. When they tell you about something unfortunate that has happened to one of their friends, ask them:
  - "Is there anything you can do to help this person feel better?"
  - "Is there anything that you could do to assist your friend?"
  - "If that was you, what would you like your friends to do?"
- Discourage negative comments about others. This also means that you should serve as an appropriate role model. Go out of your way to say something constructive about others, and make sure your children hear you.
- Teach your children the joy of giving. As a birthday present or holiday gift, give your children $5, $10, $20, or whatever you can afford, with the understanding that they should give it away. Ask them to plan and talk about the

manner in which they will donate their "gift" of money to some deserving person, group, or charity.

- Encourage your children to think about The Gift Principle discussed in this Lesson—that the most meaningful gift is the gift you *cannot* afford to give. Clearly, you must teach this principle within the context of reason—your children should never do harm to themselves in order to assist someone else.

- Encourage your children to do just one thing every day to assist another person. It could be holding a door open, allowing someone to go ahead of them in line, or giving someone a compliment. If you teach your children to be kind to others, they will cultivate friendships that can last a lifetime.

- When a loss occurs, or is anticipated, help your children explore and express their feelings about the loss. Have them draw their thoughts in pictures or write them in words. Ask them to write down the positive things that will be left behind. Help them understand that the memories of positive things can never be taken away. They will always be there.

The Three Most Difficult Decisions

C OURAGE CAN BE DEFINED AS THE MENTAL or psychological ability to resist danger or hardship. But, courage is not the same as risk-taking. Actions that give you a feeling of exhilaration, a *rush* of sorts, involve risk-taking. I have often thought of true courage as doing what you are afraid to do. But, courage is not true courage until it is tested. True courage is taking action in spite of fear. It takes courage to make difficult decisions, yet our children will be asked to make them throughout their lives. We can prepare them by helping them anticipate difficult decisions and teach them tools for better decision-making.

When faced with a difficult decision, make the best decision you can, given the information you have at the time, and then let it go. If you wait for the moment of absolute certainty, you will be paralyzed by indecision, for that moment will never arrive. Whether the decision turns out well or not, your decision will teach powerful lessons for those prepared to listen.

DECISIONS, DECISIONS

A decision is a determination or commitment to think or act in a certain way. Most of us want to make good decisions that are constructive and turn out the way we hoped they would.

Decisions, even important ones, are easier to make when:

- You have all of the relevant information you need to make the decision.
- You can change your mind and reverse your decision if you want or need to.
- The results of the decision will have minimal permanent impact on your life or the lives of others, so that, even if you are wrong, it really won't matter too much.

HomeWork

Review some of the difficult decisions you've had to make. Which of these three factors was involved?

- You had less information than you needed.
- Your decision was irrevocable.
- Your decision had a profound, irreparable effect on your life or the lives of others.

Discuss these factors with your children, and why some decisions have better outcomes than others.

Three very difficult types of decisions will face virtually all of our children during their lifetimes:

- Decisions that involve conflicts with other people
- Decisions concerning loyalty
- Decisions that involve attempting to influence or control people or things

Probably not what you were expecting, right? Let's take a closer look.

DIFFICULT DECISION #1:
Conflicts with Other People: Win–Win Decision-Making

Decision-making becomes the most complicated when other people are involved. The hardest decisions involving other people are those in which there is *conflict*. You can think of conflict as a disagreement that occurs when what you want is incompatible with what another person wants. The most important thing about resolving conflict is to keep in mind that, with every conflict comes the potential for one person to *win* and the other person to *lose*. Children can learn to reduce much of the stress associated with decisions involving a conflict with another person by using *win–win thinking*.

Let's start with the basics. Four possibilities can result from any decision your child might make that involves a conflict with another person. To make it simple, let's just think of you and me. We are faced with a decision. You want something, and I want something. But what I want is somehow incompatible with what you want. Thus, we have to make a decision that involves a conflict, because what I want *conflicts* with what you want.

Here are the possible outcomes in making any decision:

- You win, I lose. (win–lose)
- I win, you lose. (win–lose)
- You lose, I lose. (lose–lose)
- You win, I win. (win–win)

In over 30 years of professional life, one of the most important lessons I have learned is that when you win by defeating someone else, you almost never really win. There are two reasons for this.

First, if you win by taking something away from someone else, the other person almost never simply says "Okay" and let's you win. He will tend to fight back, and this can become very costly and destructive—actually more destructive than any gain that might be achieved by winning what you wanted in the first place.

Consider a dispute between two family members, Dorothy and Jane, who were fighting over how to divide an inheritance. Dorothy believed that she was entitled to a payment of $2,000 per month for three years. Jane believed that Dorothy was only entitled to receive $1,800 per month. So, the amount in dispute was $200 per month—which is a total of only $7,200 over the three-year time period. Part of the problem was that Dorothy and Jane were both competitive and did not really like one another. They could not, or would not, let the other one win.

In the end, Dorothy sued Jane and the estate for the money. Dorothy ended up spending $10,000 in legal fees in order to win an award of $7,200. Jane spent about $12,000 to defend herself against Dorothy's suit. So, who won? Would you spend $10,000 to win $7,200? Obviously, both Dorothy and Jane lost. Sounds ridiculous doesn't it? Unfortunately, this kind of thing happens every day!

Even if you win by getting what you want on the terms you asked for, you seldom really win, because the person who lost will often find a way of winning in some other way. For example, the person who lost might begin to tarnish your reputation behind your back. The person who lost might sabotage or subvert something else you want to do in the future. I can't tell you how many times I've been reminded of this from my professional "couch."

What have I said so far? The win–lose outcome almost always becomes a lose–lose situation. The cost of winning is almost always more than we bargained for, regardless of who wins.

Well, that takes care of the first three decision options listed above. What's left?: The win–win decision. This involves a decision in which both people get something positive out of it. It might not be exactly what they wanted, but there is benefit for both parties. Think of it as compromise. More importantly, you usually can't get something for yourself by keeping it from someone else. How could Dorothy and Jane have turned their fight into a win–win situation? Perhaps by compromising on the amount—say, $1,900 a month. They might not have liked each other any better, but each would have come away from the conflict feeling that she had retained some power in making the decision.

DIFFICULT DECISION #2: When to Be Loyal

Although a discussion of loyalty would seem to belong in the previous chapter on friendships and interpersonal networks, we've included it here for two reasons:

First, the question of loyalty arises, not only regarding people, but also things such as politics, religion, brands of products, and even sports teams.

Second, and most importantly, decisions about loyalty can be the most difficult ones your child will ever need to make, and the results of those decisions can change your child's life forever.

What is loyalty? According to many dictionaries, loyalty can be defined as devotion, fidelity, faithfulness, or allegiance. It might be seen as an essential element of integrity from a philosophical point of view.

Stickin' by James Carville is a wonderful book about loyalty. Carville is the brilliant political strategist who helped Bill Clinton win the Presidency and later strongly supported him during his impeachment hearing. In *Stickin'*, Carville explains his rationale for remaining faithful to President Clinton, despite the fact that Clinton lied about his sexual misconduct.

In justifying his defense of Clinton, Carville notes that some things simply do not justify abandoning a friend. Sexual misconduct, in his mind, simply did not justify turning his back on President Clinton after Clinton had befriended him and supported his career. Does this mean that we should teach our children to support a friend no matter what that friend has done? Or, should we teach our children that they must draw a line at a point beyond which they are not willing to compromise their own beliefs, values, or competing loyalties? Children and adults must learn that loyalty is a precious commodity, but that it can be misdirected, as Carville goes on to say.

> The American people treasure loyalty.... They are true to their ideals and their schools, loyal to their families and their God... [However,] Loyalty is not a virtue if it is misapplied.
>
> —JAMES CARVILLE

Children will face continuing tests of their loyalty throughout their lives. The three greatest challenges to loyalty include:

- Loyalty to one friend versus another friend
- Loyalty to friends versus parents
- Loyalty involving issues of authority and right and wrong

Loyalty is *not* a decision equipped with an "on–off" switch. There are degrees of loyalty. Citing George P. Fletcher, Carville notes that the minimum degree of loyalty one might expect is "Thou shalt not betray me." One of the greatest pains a human being will ever endure is to trust another person and to have that trust end in betrayal. The trauma of false friendships, deceptive business dealings, and extramarital affairs can last a lifetime.

Another degree of loyalty might be: "I expect you to be loyal to me whether I am right or wrong." But, as I said earlier, we all must draw a line somewhere, and there is a point at which it is more important to be true to yourself and your values than to another person. Where is that line? The sooner our children can learn to identify it, the easier conflicts of loyalty can be resolved.

HomeWork

What would you say if your teenager asked you how she should respond in a situation similar to these listed below? What would you say about these challenges to loyalty?

- Your child's best friend is suspected of cheating in school. The teacher asks your child if the friend did, in fact, cheat. What should she say if she knows her friend cheated? What if her friend did not cheat?
- Your daughter's friend, Sally, asks your daughter if she knows whether Sally's boyfriend is cheating on her. Your daughter knows that the boyfriend has been going out with another girl. Should your daughter tell Sally the truth?
- Your son's friend threw a party at his home while his parents were out of town. Underage drinking took place, and household furnishings were broken. The parents of your son's friend ask your son who was at the party. What should your son say?
- While parking her car, your daughter scratches the door of another car. She asks you if she should leave a note on the car taking responsibility for the accident. The damage would cost about $50 to repair.

- While parking her car, your daughter dents the door and fender of a new Mercedes. She asks you if she should leave a note on the car taking responsibility for the accident. The damage would cost about $5,000 to repair. If the insurance company pays for the damages, her driver's insurance premium will increase 100 percent.
- Your daughter tells you that her best friend has had an argument with the group of girls they both hang out with. Her best friend no longer wants to associate with the other girls and expects your daughter to be loyal to her and no longer hang out with them either. When you are asked what she should do, how do you respond?
- A politician, for whom you had previously voted, is impeached for sexual misconduct and lying. The politician runs for office again. Your child asks you if you are going to vote for him again. What is your decision, and how would you explain that decision to your child?

ENABLING VERSUS LOYALTY

Let's continue this theme of loyalty and push the discussion to a point at which you might not be very comfortable! Have you ever heard of "enabling?" *Enabling* behavior is when the family and friends of dishonest and disloyal people make excuses for them, cover up for them, do not hold them responsible for those actions, or simply allow them to continue being dishonest. Enabling is often seen in the families and friends of those who abuse drugs and alcohol. Enabling also commonly occurs when parents simply refuse to accept or acknowledge dishonest, disloyal, or even illegal behavior on the part of their children.

When repeated over and over again, enabling becomes ingrained as an *expectation,* both personally and culturally. The end result is that it becomes harder and harder to hold people accountable for dishonesty, disloyalty, selfish, irresponsible behavior, or even illegal behavior. When we enable children, we run the risk that they will grow up without learning to take responsibility for their actions, while always expecting someone to rescue them—or at least make excuses for them. Parental enabling often continues even after the children are grown. Sound familiar? Do you know any parents who continue to support the dishonest or disloyal behavior of their grown children? I bet you do. I do.

Enabling begins as an attempt to be protective, kind, and helpful. For example, we might make excuses for a friend who performs poorly at work or school. In doing so, we shift blame and help him avoid the disappointment of failure. But, what if that failure was deserved? What if he chose not to prepare or study? We have inadvertently rewarded irresponsible behavior and denied our friend the opportunity to learn from his mistakes.

Enabling can be confused with loyalty. Children, especially teenagers, sometimes say that to be a good friend means that you make excuses for your friends, cover up for them, and do not hold them responsible for their actions, even if those actions hurt others. As noted earlier, parents also confuse enabling with loyalty. They might say that to be a good parent means you make excuses for your children, cover up for them, and do not hold them responsible for their actions, even if those actions hurt others. Sound familiar?

As enabling behaviors become a pattern, they become expected. However, eventually we recognize the "monster" we have created and end up feeling frustrated, taken advantage of, and angry. Even then, we continue to enable those who lack integrity, and even hurt others, because we don't want to appear rude, unreasonable, or disloyal. Enabling creates a vicious cycle of never-ending problems. When we stop enabling, we become part of the solution. The decision not to enable might be the hardest decision a child—especially a teenager—will ever make. The decision *not* to enable might be the hardest decision that you as a parent may ever make.

HomeWork

Some cases in point:

1. John's son, Adam, came home from a party and told John that his watch, cell phone, and wallet had been stolen. John wanted to call the police, but Adam became very angry and said he would get them back himself. Several days later, Adam told John that he got his wallet and watch back, but all of the money was gone and his cell phone was broken. Although Adam knew who took his belongings, he refused to tell John because he did not want to get his friend in trouble. Adam said his friend was very sorry, and that he would be disloyal if he got his friend in trouble.

What would you say to Adam if he was your son?

2. Susan and Charles had been married for 20 years and had a 17-year-old daughter. Both of them had good

jobs with the government. They lived in a small, close-knit community in the Midwest. Susan was energetic and assertive; Charles was quiet and reserved. Finding the marriage lacking excitement, Charles began an affair with a woman he met on a business trip. After about a year, he told Susan that he wanted a divorce. He told her that she and their daughter were holding him back and he needed to "explore his potential, spread his wings." His wife and daughter were shocked by his desertion. His wife felt betrayed, and his daughter—who soon thereafter dyed her hair purple—said she felt abandoned.

As the holidays approached, Charles decided to have a party for his neighbors in the community as a way of introducing his new living arrangement. He had remained in the family home, and his wife and daughter moved elsewhere. Most of their neighbors were surprised when they were greeted at the door by Charles and his new girlfriend. It was clear that they were shocked by the separation. But, more clearly, there was a palpable sense of confusion about how to react. A sense of split loyalties was evident. Most of the neighbors said they wanted to remain friends with both Susan and Charles. Most interesting, perhaps, was the reaction of Charles' mother, who was a successful corporate attorney and a devout Catholic who did not believe in divorce, citing religious grounds. Later, she commented that if people are really unhappy, then divorce might be an acceptable solution. When asked what message it might send to her granddaughter, she abruptly said, "I can't think about that now."

Having just read about Susan and Charles, what do you think?

- Were the neighbors enabling or loyal by staying at the party and acting as if nothing had changed?
- Were the neighbors enabling or loyal for wanting to remain friends with both Susan and Charles?
- Was Charles' mother enabling or loyal because she changed her mind about divorce on the basis of her son's current situation?
- If your child was a friend of Susan's daughter, what would you tell her to say when Susan's daughter expressed her anger at her father and his girlfriend?

A KING, A KID, AND A BASEBALL GAME

Although this event took place when my son was 17, I didn't tell him about it until one night at a family dinner seven years later. I had been working in a country that had been ravaged by war. My efforts lasted many years, and I had made many friends in the government and in the royal family that ruled the country. On one particular trip, I received a message that I was going to meet with the King to be formally thanked for my efforts. This was quite an honor.

At the last moment, I was told that our meeting would need to be rescheduled because a conflict had arisen. The ceremony was now scheduled for a day when I was supposed to be back in the

United States. For five or six years in a row, my father and my son had a ritual of going to Opening Day for the Baltimore Orioles. It just so happened that the ceremony with His Highness was scheduled for the same day.

The challenge for me was to determine where my greatest loyalty resided. It took me only three seconds to realize that I needed to pass up the professional opportunity of a lifetime to be with my son and my father. I turned down the remarkable honor that had been offered as politely as I could. The shock on the royal representative's face was a sight to behold. He could not believe I was turning down the invitation. I could hardly believe it myself, and mentioned my decision to no one.

Opening Day arrived, and my father and I drove to my son's school to pick him up to go to the ballpark. My son met us, disappointment evident on his face, and said that he had a baseball game that day at school. His coach had told him that he could not miss the team's opening day. My son had worked hard to earn a starting position at second base.

It was decided that the three of us would attend my son's opening game. I have not had one moment of regret for my decision to miss the meeting with His Highness on Opening Day for the Baltimore Orioles, because to remain loyal to my work seemed less important in comparison to the loyalty I felt to my father and my son. Easy decision, right?

DIFFICULT DECISION #3: The Issue of Control

The topic of control might seem out of place in a book on parenting, but in fact it's both relevant and very important. For years, my clinical practice focused on treating people who had so much stress in their lives that it was making them physically sick. As I saw more and more of these patients, it became clear to me that many of them suffered from the same problem: They had difficulty making decisions about control.

These people were experiencing extremely high levels of stress because they lived their lives in such a way that they continually tried to control people or things over which they had no actual control. As a result, they wasted precious time and energy. They never seemed to live up to their potential in anything they tried. The irony was that their frustration and anger ultimately controlled them by making them sick and limiting their overall health, professional growth, and happiness. We can teach our children a powerful lesson about how to best use their time and energy by not wasting it on things over which they have no control.

The "Yes" Sickness

Have you ever met someone who can never seem to say "no," and says "yes" to everything? At first, you were probably impressed, but later felt frustrated because these people always become overcommitted and highly stressed, and seldom complete jobs they promise to do or live up to their commitments. This leads to strained relationships with co-workers and friends, even family. Why? People with the "yes" sickness are actually *afraid* to say "no," because they think they will miss an opportunity or—worse yet—disappoint someone.

Responsibility Without Authority: The "Kiss of Death?"

Students in business schools are taught that the worst job a person can possibly have is one with great responsibility but without the authority to see that the job gets done. The most stressful jobs on Earth are those in which there is a high level of responsibility but little authority and a low ability to control outcomes.

Tom was a 27-year-old single man who was referred to me by his family physician. He suffered from life-threatening colitis (inflammation of the colon). His gastroenterologist had scheduled him for a colostomy, a surgical procedure that involves connecting a part of the colon to the abdominal wall, leaving an opening called a *stoma*. After a colostomy, waste exits the patient's body through the stoma and collects in a pouch worn on the outside of the body. For a single 27-year-old man, this was a very serious operation that everyone wanted to avoid, especially Tom.

Tom's doctors were convinced that stress was causing his colitis. It soon became obvious that they were correct. This young man and his uncle had inherited a successful construction business. Tom's job was to give customers estimates for work the company proposed to do. It was very important that the estimates were accurate. Tom also had to promise that the work would be completed by a certain date; if the job was completed late, the cost would be deducted from the company's profits. So far, so good. The problem was that Tom's time and cost estimates relied upon his uncle, who was in charge of getting the materials to complete the job. Unfortunately, Tom's uncle was not very good at his job, and he did not seem to care as much about the success of the company as Tom did. As a result, Tom's time and cost estimates were almost never accurate. This made Tom look bad to his customers, and it was costly to the company.

In other words, Tom was responsible for the jobs being completed in a timely and profitable manner, but he did not have the authority to make it happen. This situation was not only costly in terms of dollars, it also was costly in terms of Tom's health.

We were able to prevent Tom from undergoing surgery by teaching him techniques to handle the factors he could not control and that were causing his stress. We also showed Tom how to restructure his job in relation to that of his uncle's. But, that's a subject for a different book!

The Answer to Excessive Control: Serenity

Four factors need to be considered in relation to the great dilemma of when to exert control—and when to accept particular circumstances in your life:

God, give us grace to accept with serenity the things that cannot be changed, courage to change the things that should be changed, and the wisdom to distinguish the one from the other.

—*THE SERENITY PRAYER*

Give us the serenity to accept the things that cannot be changed, courage to change the things that should be changed, and the wisdom to know that the only thing we can really change is ourselves.

—*ANOTHER VERSION OF THE SERENITY PRAYER*

- *Mastery.* When you attempt to influence or control something over which you can actually achieve some significant degree of control, the process can result in mastery.
- *Frustration.* When you attempt to influence something over which you have no actual ability to achieve control, the process can result in frustration, a sense of futility, and perhaps even anger (sound familiar?).
- *Letting go.* When you decide NOT to attempt to influence something over which you can actually achieve control, the process is called *letting go.*
- *Serenity.* When you recognize things over which you have no control, and then decide NOT to waste time and energy attempting to influence them, the process is called *serenity.*

What does this have to do with raising children? Simple. The ability to recognize the people and things in life over which we have no influence or control is one of the greatest attributes your children can develop. It saves time, energy, and frustration, and leads to more efficient and effective lives. In simple terms, teach your children not to waste their time trying to control people and things that cannot be controlled.

HomeWork

- We started this chapter by telling you that the three most difficult decisions your child will ever have to make are:
  - Decisions that involve conflicts with other people
  - Decisions concerning loyalty
  - Decisions that involve attempting to influence or control the people or things around you
- The next time your child has a conflict with another person, sit down and discuss the situation with your child. Take the opportunity to explain the principles of a *win–win* decision. Ask how the situation might be handled in order to have a positive outcome for everyone involved. Discuss how similar situations in the future might be handled. Explain to your child that compromise is not giving in, but rather the recognition that other people have needs and desires that might be as valid as his own, and therefore warrant consideration.
- Find an opportunity to discuss the concept of loyalty with your child. Perhaps something in the news could prompt the discussion. (Election season is a great opportunity to discuss issues of honesty and loyalty!) During the course of the discussion, consider two or three situations that might challenge the concept of loyalty. More important than *what* your child might do, ask him *why* he might make a particular decision.

- When you see your child acting "irrationally," it's helpful to point it out. For example, if you observe him trying to control someone or something that cannot be controlled, ask him if he "really" expected things to change. If so, why? Also, questions such as, "Dad, how do I get girls to like me?" set the stage not only for practical dating suggestions, but for the realization that a person can do everything right and still not "get the girl."

Teach Your Children to Take Responsibility for Their Actions

DID YOU EVER MEET A PERSON WHO SIMPLY refused to accept responsibility for something he did that went wrong or that ended up being a poor choice? Perhaps you tried to point out his mistake in a constructive way, but the person became angry, accused you of being critical, and generally tried to blame you. Makes you crazy, doesn't it? Believe it or not, this type of person simply never grew up. Generally speaking, their lives are long journeys of self-doubt, disappointment, and regret, punctuated by periods of selfishness and angry tirades. Much of this can be traced back to a failure to learn to take responsibility and parents who never helped them mature as human beings.

I'll never forget an incident that occurred one day while I was shopping. I was standing in the checkout line when a woman came back to the store wanting to return a movie video tape. She told the clerk that she had accidentally recorded over the movie on the tape and wanted a new one.

What you do today will echo for eternity.

—MAXIMUS (FROM THE MOVIE *GLADIATOR*)

The clerk said, "I'm sorry; I don't understand." He seemed as confused as I was. The woman quickly interrupted, and in a loud and aggressive voice said, "Well, you're not saying this was my fault are you? After all, there should have been a notice on the tape telling me not to record over the movie!"

Before the clerk could respond, the store manager, who had overheard the discussion, came over, apologized, and gave the woman another tape, free of charge. I suppose his actions would be considered good business, but it made me a little angry because the woman was obviously not taking responsibility for ruining the tape.

You cannot escape the responsibility of tomorrow by evading it today.
—ABRAHAM LINCOLN

Taking responsibility for your actions is simple, so why don't more people do it? Somehow, children learn that they have the prerogative, if not the obligation, to find someone to blame when something goes wrong. We blame our parents, our teachers, our employers, or the great conspiracy promulgated by the opposing political party.

It seems to me the world would be a far better place if only people would take responsibility for their actions. Avoiding responsibility appears to be a culturally adopted value. Why so? Taking responsibility for your actions when you have made a mistake can affect your self-esteem. Simply said, taking responsibility for your actions when you make a mistake says you were wrong, you did a poor job, you were less than competent on that endeavor. These words are poison to our ears, especially if you were raised in the "I'm okay; you're okay" generation, or if you were raised in the generation in which everyone got a trophy for winning and there were never any losers.

There can be no freedom without responsible living.
—THOMAS JEFFERSON

THE MEANING OF A MISTAKE

Mistakes are embarrassing, and they can be expensive. Mistakes make us question ourselves. Taking responsibility for your mistakes is much easier when you realize that isolated actions, such as accidents and one-time misjudgments or miscalculations, are not *who* you are, they are simply *what* you did. Only when you repeat the same actions—especially if you know what the outcome will be—are they a reflection of *who* you are.

Remember the people who can't stand criticism, and who can't take responsibility? These are people who tell themselves, "I am my mistakes." What they do not understand is that—for the most part—taking responsibility for your actions when things have not turned out well is not only *not* a sign of weakness, but a sign of strength and integrity. It is recognizing

> *Character—the willingness to accept responsibility for one's own life—is the source from which self-respect springs.*
>
> –Joan Didion

that no one is perfect. It *is* a statement about who you are—it says you have integrity and courage, and that you are concerned about people and things other than yourself.

People who continually blame others for their mistakes generally have very poor self-esteem, but where does that poor self-esteem come from? That's right: parents who continually criticize and second-guess their children, and send direct and indirect messages to their children that their best is not quite good enough. These parents tend to raise children with poor self-esteem, who suffer a lifetime of insecurity. Worse yet, their kids perpetuate the legacy of insecurity by passing it on to their own children. Just as nothing was good enough for their parents, nothing will be good enough for them. Isn't part of our job as parents to teach our children self-respect? To do this, we must teach our children to take responsibility.

You can't keep blaming yourself. Just blame yourself once, and move on.
–HOMER SIMPSON

Here's another twist: Consider parents who are *too* supportive of their children, too enmeshed in their children's lives (remember the enabling parent?). These parents think their children can do no wrong and, when the kids fail to live up to parental expectations, their coaches and teachers are blamed. Once again, the children are taught not to take responsibility for their actions.

Most of us would agree that we want our children to learn self-respect. But, how in the world are they going to learn it if we keep telling them that they are not responsible for anything they do, bad or good? It works both ways, you know.

RESPONSIBILITY AND THE FAMILY

Most people have two families: their family of origin (the family they are born into), and their family of procreation (the family they create when they have their own children).

Children begin to learn responsibility for their actions by learning that they are part of something larger than themselves—a family. They need to learn that the family can be a source of support, but they also need to learn a sense of responsibility to their family. Not only do your actions reflect on you, they reflect on your family. Children should strive to avoid doing anything that reflects badly on the people they love and who love them. When these children grow into adults, they will have learned to avoid things that bring shame or hurt to their parents, spouses, and children. Oh, what a wonderful world it would be! Wasn't there a song about this?

When your children look back over their lives, what will their legacy be? Will they look back with pride? Will they say they were good role models, or will they look back with regret? Will their legacy be one of excuses? The answer to those questions begins with YOU and what you teach them about accepting responsibility.

TAKING RESPONSIBILITY: A CASE IN POINT

A 50-year-old surgeon sought treatment for depression after one of his patients died during surgery, apparently as a direct result of his actions. The surgeon blamed himself for not being more conservative. He also believed he should have done a more thorough job of explaining the risks of surgery to the patient and her family. Initially, he was so distressed that he contemplated retiring from the practice of medicine. He felt he had betrayed a trust placed in him by the patient and her family. Fortunately, his depression began to lift after several sessions in therapy.

HomeWork

Here's the hard part...if you were to die tomorrow, what would be your legacy? How would you be remembered? Take a moment and write that on a piece of paper.

Now, look at the words you just wrote. Are you satisfied that the time and energy you have expended over the course of your life so far has created a legacy of which you are proud, of which your children would be proud? It's never too late to alter your legacy you know.

One of the key aspects of his recovery was not making excuses or blaming the patient's age on the poor outcome, but instead taking responsibility. He decided to write this patient's case up, present it to all incoming students, and publish it in a medical journal. He wrote about how his actions had led to the patient's death, even though it was potentially embarrassing. He explained that he did this in hopes that the students would do a better job with their patients than he believed he had done with this particular patient.

The practice of health care is always challenging, but what happens when you make a mistake? Should you admit it, say you are sorry, and offer a remedy? Should you try to cover it up, blame someone else, or simply not talk about it and hope it will go away?

Studies show that the most important factor in people's decisions to file lawsuits is not negligence, but ineffective communication between patients and providers. Malpractice suits often result when an unexpected adverse outcome is met with a lack of empathy from physicians and a perceived or actual withholding of essential information.
–NEW ENGLAND JOURNAL OF MEDICINE

For years, not talking about unfortunate outcomes in the treatment of patients was common in the practice of medicine, but this attitude inadvertently seemed to fuel the tort-oriented legal system. More recently, there has been a movement to encourage full disclosure of health care–related mistakes and encourage apologies. Has this new attitude been a success? It might be too early to tell, but the early returns are encouraging.

According to data reported from the University of Michigan Health System at www.SorryWorks.net, a reduction in legal costs by as much as one-third can result when health care facilities admit mistakes and disclose all important information to patients or their families.

According to Christine Koentopp, Director of Pharmacy at Children's Hospitals and Clinics in Minneapolis, there has been a nearly 50 percent decline in malpractice lawsuits since it began a full disclosure program regarding medical errors. The program is called *Ops* (oops).

In an October, 2007, brief from the American Psychiatric Association, the concept of taking responsibility for one's actions is framed within the context of an apology after a medical mistake. The brief notes, "Some commentators argue that silence or denial after a medical or clinical mistake can lead to a greater risk of a lawsuit.... Patients want caregivers to acknowledge the incident and explain what happened. If an error occurred, patients want someone to take responsibility and also often ensure that the same thing doesn't happen to someone else." The brief goes on to say that, "Denial of culpability also leads to a betrayal of the patient's or client's trust."

If we take this out of the medical context, it provides wise insight about the message we teach our children and might read like something like this:

- Teach your children to accept responsibility for their actions.
- Teach your children that to deny responsibility is dishonest, and that such a denial of responsibility can be seen as a betrayal of trust that someone else has given them.
- Teach them that remaining silent or using denial after making a mistake can lead to greater anger or frustration on the part of the person you have hurt. People simply want someone to admit that the incident occurred and explain what happened. They just want someone to take responsibility.

SELF-RESPONSIBILITY BUILDS INNER STRENGTH:
Carpe Diem, Carpe Vita

Taking responsibility for your actions should just be plain old common sense. But, it must start with *you*, the parents of the next generation. If you teach your children to hide from responsibility and embrace excuses, you condemn them to a life of poor self-esteem that will be marked by powerlessness, dependency, and the constant search for someone to blame. These qualities ultimately create a chronic negativism and, ultimately, regret for a life not fully lived, a future never completely realized.

Common sense is the collection of prejudices acquired by age eighteen.
–ALBERT EINSTEIN

Acceptance of what has happened is the first step in overcoming misfortune.
–WILLIAM JOYCE

On the other hand, if you teach your children to take responsibility for their actions and their lives, you actually empower them to grow. It's risky, yes. But, what truly valuable things in life are risk-free? By teaching your children to take responsibility, you teach them to take control of their lives, and you empower them to seize opportunities rather fear or run away from them.

Carpe diem is the Latin phrase for "seize the day." Perhaps it should be *carpe vita*, "seize life." You do that by accepting responsibility.

EMPOWERMENT IS NOT ENOUGH: Persistence Is Needed

Yes, responsibility empowers, but it's not enough. Once your children have been empowered to act, they must learn the importance of *perseverance*, which means not giving up simply because the task at hand becomes difficult. This is not to say that talent, genius, and education are not important, they are—but perseverance and determination are more important.

One of my roommates in college was a remarkable salesman. I knew he was destined for great things. As our senior year was ending, we were enrolled in a retail marketing class. He seemed in his glory. I asked him if he thought I had a future in sales. Rather emphatically, he said "No!"

Although I must say my feelings were hurt, I asked him why. He asked me how many rejections from potential customers it would take before I became frustrated. I told him four or five. He just laughed. Somewhat annoyed, I asked him how many rejections it would take before he became really frustrated. I'll never forget his answer, "If there were 100 potential customers, and I've gotten 99 rejections, the way I would look at it is that I have one more chance." Today, my former roommate is financially successful, a community leader, and a man dedicated to his family and friends. He remains one of the most tenacious people I've ever known.

Press on! Nothing in the world can take the place of perseverance. Talent will not; nothing is more common than unsuccessful men with talent. Genius will not; unrewarded genius is almost a proverb. Education will not; the world is full of educated derelicts. Persistence and determination alone are omnipotent.
—Calvin Coolidge

Calvin Coolidge and Winston Churchill exemplified the importance of perseverance. At the time British Prime Minister Winston Churchill spoke the famous words "Never give in," the Second World War was not going well for Great Britain. Denmark, Norway, France, Belgium, Luxembourg, and The Netherlands had all fallen to invading German forces. Great Britain had been subjected to massive bombing from July 1940 to May 1941. At one point, London was bombed for 57 consecutive nights. By the time the bombing stopped, over 43,000 civilians had been killed and more than a million homes destroyed or damaged, leaving hundreds of thousands of people homeless.

Churchill realized that the greatest resource his country had was its people, and that their greatest strength was their will to endure and persevere. He took every opportunity to bolster their spirits and to reinforce the notion that you are beaten the moment you *think* that you are beaten—and not before. Their persistence and willingness to endure the terrible bombings ultimately forced Germany to give up its plans to invade Great Britain.

But, for everyone...
this is the lesson:
Never give in.
Never give in.
Never, never, never,
never, in nothing,
great or small,
large or petty.
Never give in,
except to convictions
of honour and good
sense. Never yield
to force. Never yield
to the apparently
overwhelming might
of the enemy.
–WINSTON CHURCHILL

What message do you want to give your children? It seems to me that we have an obligation as parents to encourage our children not to give up, even though life can become very difficult at times. We need to teach them that the likelihood of being defeated is greatly increased if you *already believe* you are defeated. But, we also need to teach what Shakespeare felt was equally important: *discretion is the better part of valor.* There's the challenge! When is it actually a good idea to stop and walk away, and not feel like a quitter? When is it best to walk away because, even though you have tried, you simply cannot achieve the end result you want? I guess in many instances the answer is when the emotional and/or financial cost of persevering, even when you win, becomes greater than the cost of walking away.

THE CONSEQUENCES OF NOT TEACHING SELF-RESPONSIBILITY

Do you remember the so-called "McDonald's coffee case"…*Liebeck v. McDonald's Restaurants?* This lawsuit became a virtual icon for frivolous lawsuits. ABC News even called it "the poster child of excessive lawsuits." A jury awarded $2.9 million to Stella Liebeck, a 79-year-old woman who burned herself with hot coffee purchased at a McDonald's restaurant. The trial judge reduced the total award to $640,000, and the parties later settled for an undisclosed amount thought to be less than $600,000. This case became a popular example for those who thought any reasonable person should have known that coffee labeled "hot" would indeed be hot, and should have taken responsibility to handle it carefully.

I believe that common sense *is* common, and it's available to those who choose to use it. But we give our children a host of reasons to *not* use it. The socially instilled, virtual obligation to escape responsibility is one such reason. Combine the socially promoted, parentally supported obligation to escape taking responsibility for actions with a legal system that rewards the abandonment of rational thought (common sense), and you have a society that no longer expects its members to act responsibly. If society doesn't expect you to act in a responsible manner, why should you? As a result, we end up with consumer product warnings that serve to tell us a lot about the culture we have created. Consider the following overly obvious warning labels for those who have suspended rational thought in favor of adopting a helpless lack of responsibility—what do they say about us as a culture?

> *Common sense ain't common.*
> –WILL ROGERS

- Warning on a hair dryer: "Never use hair dryer while sleeping."
- Warning on a toilet brush: "Do not use toilet brush for personal hygiene."
- Warning on an electric iron: "Never iron clothes while they are being worn."
- Warning on a can of pepper spray used for self-defense: "Pepper spray may irritate eyes."
- Warning on a thermometer: "Once used rectally, the thermometer should not be used orally."
- Warning on a knife: "Never try to catch a falling knife."
- Warning on a bag of microwave popcorn: "Do not reuse bag."
- Warning on deodorant: "For external use only."
- Warnings on a *children's* anti-allergy medication: "Do not use if pregnant or breast-feeding. Avoid alcoholic beverages. Be careful

if driving a motor vehicle or operating machinery." How many children do you know that do *any* of these things?

I could not verify this last example, but I thought I'd pass it along:

• Warning on a Swedish chain saw: "Do not attempt to stop chain with your hands or genitals."

THE FAILURE TO TEACH RESPONSIBILITY CAN LAST A LIFETIME

Kathy was the youngest of nine children. Her father died when she was 4 years old. She grew up with a mother and eight siblings looking over her shoulder and evaluating everything she did. Times were difficult, and there was no room for waste or inefficiency. Kathy was very active in sports and other activities, mostly to stay away from her very critical family.

In an effort to escape, she married young and had four children. Her first child was a daughter named Claudia. Initially, things were fine. But, as more children followed, things changed. Kathy had to rely on Claudia to help her raise the younger children. As much as she swore she would never do to her children what her family had done to her, she became very critical. On one hand, she gave Claudia a lot of responsibility, but she was always critical and second-guessing. So, in reality, Claudia was given pseudo-responsibility—a false sense of responsibility, similar to our previous discussion of responsibility in business.

As you might imagine, Claudia's self-esteem was badly beaten down by this pseudo-responsibility. She learned that the only way to escape her mother's constant criticism was to make excuses and blame others. Her friends jokingly called her "Teflon Claudia" because she would never allow criticism to stick. She was a master at blaming others. Claudia became a very negative person, beautiful and affable on the surface, but avoidant and negative under-neath. For Claudia, the glass was always half empty. She even developed *passive-aggressive* ways of relating to others, which is when one person criticizes another, but does so in an indirect way that is hard to detect as a direct insult or criticism. This might occur by way of so-called *backhanded compliments*, as we discussed earlier.

Claudia was never taught how to take responsibility for her actions in a positive constructive environment; she was never given the authority that should have gone along with responsibility. She was never allowed to mature psychologically. Her self-esteem was so poor, she was never truly happy.

What happened to Claudia? She became pregnant at age 17, and again at age 19. Both pregnancies were aborted. Claudia began a high-powered career after earning an MBA degree, not because she really wanted to, but because she thought it was required. She constantly questioned herself in everything she did, both person-ally and professionally. She became bitter and selfish.

Although she never expected to, Claudia finally married, although she ended up marrying a man with whom she had previously had an affair. She had four children of her own, not because she wanted to, but because she thought it was expected. She loved her children, but she resented the time and energy they demanded. Her frustration grew to the point where she would explode into angry tirades. She was disrespectful and verbally abusive to her husband.

When Claudia reached 40, she experienced a mid-life crisis. Some might call it a "melt down." You know—one of those crises where you see your life unfolding in a way you never expected or never wanted. Claudia felt as if time was running out. She began to have panic attacks. She viewed her children and her husband as lia-bilities that kept her from realizing her potential. To rationalize her resentment of her children and her husband, Claudia said that they were holding her back, keeping her from spreading her wings. In desperation, Claudia changed her life. She underwent radical plastic surgery, had an affair, and left her family. Claudia had grown up to become a toxic person, so much so that even her children recognized it and distanced themselves from her.

What does Claudia's story teach us about child-rearing? First, children will grow to their potential if you give them responsibility, but you must also give them the authority to get the job done within an atmosphere of support and constructive feedback. Praise successes, while constructively pointing how to correct mistakes. Always focus critiques on the actions, not the child. As for a lesson for children themselves, they should learn to critique the actions of people, not the people themselves.

HomeWork

Here are some steps you and your children can take to bring focus and understanding to the concepts discussed in Lesson #3. Tools are included to help kids learn to take responsibility for their actions.

- Be a role model for your children. Take responsibility for *your* actions as a way of teaching them that they should take responsibility for theirs. When you make a mistake, acknowledge it, and then try to come up with a solution. Remember, your children are constantly watching and learning from your actions.

- Most people have difficulty accepting compliments, especially children. Good grief, not only can't we accept responsibility for the things that go wrong, we can't even accept responsibility for the things that go right! When someone compliments you, what do you say? Perhaps your typical response is "Oh, it was nothing." By saying these words, you have just dismissed both the compliment *and* the person who made it. You've also reduced your chances of getting another compliment. Practice giving your children compliments (but only when warranted; unwarranted compliments feed another problem called *entitlement*) and help them practice accepting them. Simple statements such as "Thank you," or in response to some performance, "Thank you, I really tried" or "Thank you, I was happy with my effort" might be useful. As your children become more comfortable accepting compliments from you, they will feel less uncomfortable accepting compliments from others. This ultimately communicates confidence.
- Now the hard part: Help your children admit to themselves and others when things do not go well. Teach them to use phrases such as:
  - "I hoped to do better."
  - "I was disappointed."
  - "I think I can do better."
  - "I need to do a better job preparing next time."

When good just isn't good enough, they might simply say:

-"I did the best I could; it just wasn't good enough this time."

Harder yet, when they make a mistake, teach them to do two things:

-Say "I'm sorry;" and

-Ask the question (within reason), "What can I do to fix it" or "What can I do to make up for my mistake?"

Be sure to teach your children that acknowledging a problem or mistake is not the same as making excuses. You can also teach them that an occasional mistake or failure is what they *did*, not who they *are*.

Simply acknowledging mistakes doesn't necessarily excuse them. You don't want to raise a child who is careless in her behavior because she thinks a simple "I was wrong; I'm sorry" is all that's needed to clear the slate. You need to teach your kids that sometimes specific actions are needed to right a wrong.

- This might sound silly, but put up a simple 3 × 5 index card in plain sight with the words, "What I do today is my legacy for tomorrow" on it. A simple reminder like this can serve to remind us that life is about more than ourselves; it's about the mosaic of life experiences we leave behind and how that mosaic affects those whose lives we have touched. It's not about YOU! It's about US.
- Put up a sign that says "NO EXCUSES" in a place where your children will see it on a regular basis.

Discuss the meaning of the sign with them. Let them know you will remind them when you notice they are making excuses for their behavior and not taking responsibility. "The dog ate my homework" is not going to work anymore!

- Teach your child perseverance by having them ask this question after they complete a task: "Is this the best I can do?" If not, teach the child to go back and give it one additional effort, but initially only *one* additional effort. We must teach our children to strive for excellence, not perfection. Otherwise, we risk creating people such as Kathy and Claudia, for whom nothing is ever quite good enough.

- Finally, a few words about "time versus intensity." When I was 25 years old, I was an avid weightlifter. I went to the gym 4 days a week and did some other form of exercise the remaining days. One day, while I was speaking to the gym manager, I commented that the gym seemed more crowded than usual. He said, "Yeah, we're running a lifetime membership special— a one-time fee of $400."

  "How can you do that?" I said. "You'll have to sell thousands of memberships just to stay in business. What happens if everyone decides to use the club at the same time?"

  He laughed and said it would never happen. "Most people join a gym and work out every day for a while, but then they get tired of it and quit. They don't understand that the key to successfully meeting your goals in physical exercise is time, not intensity."

What he was trying to tell me was that the key to successful physical exercise, or any other goal, is persistence—adopting a routine you can do comfortably and staying with it. I think life is like that, isn't it? The mistake we often make is expecting too much, too soon. We give up before we can even begin to realize our goals.

So, teach your children that if they want something badly enough, they should take the first step, then another, and then another. With time, they may just reach their goal. But also teach them that a successful journey means taking responsibility along the way.

Making the Most Important Investment of a Lifetime: Invest in Your Health

WE ARE TOLD THAT WE SHOULD TEACH our children at an early age how to save and invest financially. Investing money at an early age is sound advice, but how about teaching children to invest in something even more important than finances: their health. The best investment you can make is in your health. You've heard it so many times before: Without good health, nothing else you possess really matters. Let's explore this intriguing topic.

We spend the first half of our lives sacrificing our health in order to gain wealth, we then spend the second half of our lives sacrificing our wealth in order to regain our health.

PROMOTING HEALTH BEFORE TREATING DISEASE

The last century saw two fundamental shifts related to health. The first was a change in the causes of death in the United States. The second was the emergence of how we pursue health. Let's take a closer look.

In the first half of the twentieth century, Americans died from germ-based communicable diseases, such as influenza and pneumonia, but in the latter half of the century they began to die from degenerative diseases, such as heart disease, cancer, and stroke, as well as from accidents, especially motor vehicle accidents.

In the 1970s, we witnessed a fundamental shift in the pursuit of health, with the emergence of the age of wellness and health promotion. This represented a change in priorities related to the delivery of health care services. The emphasis had been on early detection and aggressive treatment of illness, but the age of wellness heralded the advent of the promotion of *wellness*. Wellness is not simply the absence of disease. It's the pursuit of higher and longer-lasting functional well-being. It is important to note that, despite the fact that medical science has extended the average lifespan, we have failed to extend the *functional* lifespan. This means that we are living longer but enjoying it less.

The age of wellness has taught us that many of the choices we make can dramatically affect our health. Health-related behaviors can either erode health or support it. Many public health authorities agree that a significant factor in the cause of the diseases of the twentieth century is our lifestyle, meaning the choices you make about how you live. Shouldn't we teach our children how to make good lifestyle decisions—how to act in such a way so as to promote their health? In doing so, they will invest most wisely.

THE HEALTH PROMOTION PYRAMID

One way to look at how your children can learn to promote health is the health promotion pyramid, which has four major components:

- Exercise: How you use your body
- Nutrition: How you refuel your body

- Sleep and Rest: How much time you allow your body to spend repairing and rebuilding itself after daily "wear and tear"
- Attitude: The way you choose to view yourself and the world around you.

INVESTING IN YOURSELF: THE HEALTH PROMOTION PYRAMID

Physical exercise is the peak of the pyramid for two reasons:

- Exercise allows your children to constructively express themselves, especially emotionally.
- Most importantly, exercise is at the peak of the pyramid because it is the only reliable way your children's bodies can grow stronger.

Nutrition is the second tier, because it fuels exercise and everything else your children do at home, at school, and at play.

Rest and sleep is the third tier, because in order for your children's bodies to benefit from exercise and nutrition, there must be a time during the day when the body's highest priority is repair and growth.

Finally, all of these traditional health-related factors rest on the most important element in the health promotion pyramid—attitude. Unless they are motivated to exercise while they are young, your children will tend to not exercise as they grow older. Unless they understand the value of eating certain foods or taking vitamins, they will tend not to do so. Unless your children realize the importance of getting adequate rest, they will tend to get less than they need, especially during their teenage and young adult years.

Realizing the importance of health-promoting factors and making good choices is all about attitude. But, attitude affects health in another way—a positive attitude promotes less stress than a negative attitude. This includes the manner in which children are taught to interpret successes and failures in life. Let's take a closer look at the four elements of the health promotion pyramid.

PHYSICAL EXERCISE

Let's start with exercise. The health-promoting effects of exercise have been well known for centuries:

- Physical exercise is one important way children and adults can express their feelings, such as joy, frustration, anger, and depression. After exercise, people usually report feeling calmer and more relaxed. My oldest daughter made physical exercise an essential aspect of her life. Growing up, it was easy for me to tell when she had not exercised, because she seemed more irritable. I have noticed the same thing about myself. Physical exercise has even been used as part of a treatment plan for depression.
- Exercise strengthens the body. For example, your muscles will become larger and stronger with weight-lifting. The cardiopulmonary system can be strengthened with cardiovascular endurance exercise. Recent animal studies show that exercise

actually helps the regeneration of damaged brain circuits, and it might help facilitate learning and memory function.

• Exercise burns calories and can assist in dieting, weight management, and even reshaping your physical appearance.

• Exercise has an interpersonal benefit, too. By *interpersonal* I mean that exercising with other people can become a social outlet. Perhaps even more importantly for children, team sports can help teach essential life skills about how to work with others, how to cope with success, and how to cope with failure. A useful guide to using team sports as a way to develop these qualities can be found in *Dr. Rob's Guide to Raising Fit Kids: A Family-Centered Approach to Achieving Optimal Health* (DiaMedica, 2008).

Lack of regular physical exercise has been theorized to be the source of many degenerative and stress-related diseases. We know that there appears to be a virtual epidemic of obesity among children in the United States, an epidemic that is certainly fueled by a lack of physical exercise. Let's take a closer look at the different ways to exercise.

Types of Exercise

There are two types of exercise: aerobic and anaerobic. *Aerobic* exercise is what we typically think of as endurance exercise. Activities such as jogging, running, soccer, biking, and even brisk walking increase your heart rate while you are performing them and build endurance.

Anaerobic exercises, such as weightlifting, golf, and bowling, tend to build muscular strength and skill. A good exercise program should include both aerobic and anaerobic exercises. After being cleared by a physician, it is usually recommended that you exercise for at least 30 minutes a day and a minimum of three days per week.

Benefits of Exercise

Exercise is a powerful tool to help build life skills and resiliency. We've already mentioned some of the benefits, but here is an expanded list. Exercise can:

- Improve cardiopulmonary (heart and lung) efficiency
- Improve sugar utilization
- Reduce body fat
- Reduce resting blood pressure
- Reduce muscle tension
- Reduce anxiety
- Reduce depression
- Improve self-esteem
- Improve interpersonal skills
- With team sports, improve the ability to live and work in groups

The key to building a life-long habit of exercise is to start early. Teach your children that exercise is a way of life, not just something to do on an as-needed basis—such as exercising in January to take off the five pounds you put on over the holidays.

Here's a final tip about exercise. The most important part of exercise is not how hard you work out; rather, it's how *long* you work out. It's better to exercise for 30 minutes with moderate exertion than to work out for 15 minutes with maximum exertion. It's better to pick a workout schedule that you will keep for a year, even if it's less intense than something you might do just in the spring to get in shape for summer. Perseverance is the key. For kids, as well as adults, it's important to make exercise fun and to exercise with other people—social support is essential for long-term commitment.

NUTRITION

Someone once said *you are what you eat.* I remember eating a lot of Twinkies and Spam. Hmm…Oh well. We do know that food plays an important role in resiliency and health in general. Not only is what you eat and drink the fuel that creates energy for your body, it's the building blocks of life—it's how your body repairs itself and grows. Food can also be a source of *instant* energy.

Balanced Nutrition

Most authorities will tell you that it is important to eat a balanced diet, and we certainly agree. Your children need sugars, fats, and especially proteins, but this is not a book about childhood nutrition, so we'll leave the in-depth discussion of this topic for others. There are a few things we would like to mention, however, with the important note that choosing or dramatically changing a nutritional program should never be done without consulting a qualified professional.

Vitamins, Minerals, and Herbs

Vitamins are nutrients required in small quantities that cannot be made by the body but that are needed for optimal function. Some vitamins are especially important for resiliency and resisting stress. Water-soluble vitamins, such as vitamin C and the B group of vitamins, are depleted at a faster rate when you are under stress. Stress-formula vitamins are largely made up of these vitamins on the assumption that stress can lead to deficiencies of them.

In the last five years or so, vitamins and minerals have been marketed on the assumption that they enhance the immune system and improve your body's ability to resist and be resilient to infectious illnesses such colds and influenza. A variety of products that include vitamins, minerals, and herbs said to aid physical resistance and resilience are popular; however, whether such products actually reduce the prevalence and severity of colds and influenza remains beyond the scope of this discussion.

There is some concern that Americans might be taking too many vitamin supplements. It has been said we have the most expensive urine in the world, because we take these substances in such excessive amounts that our bodies simply excrete them. Some experts believe that foods contain the necessary vitamins and minerals and, if we take supplements, we are simply wasting our money. The problem with this argument is that it makes several unfounded assumptions:

- It assumes that most people eat balanced, healthy meals. How many children—especially adolescents—do you know who eat truly balanced diets, complete with all the necessary vitamins and minerals?
- It assumes that naturally occurring vitamins and minerals are not depleted or altered when foods are processed or prepared for eating.
- It assumes that vitamins and minerals cannot exert their own health-promoting effects independent of their interaction with the foods we eat.

Over-the-counter drugs, herbs, and vitamins should only be used in consultation with a knowledgeable physician. This is especially true when children are the consumers.

Stimulants: Instant Energy

Food is converted into energy through a process called *metabolism*. Sugars and fats fuel living cells. Another way of getting energy that does not rely on what we think of as traditional foods is through the use of stimulants. We often think of stimulants as drugs that are obtained through a physician or pharmacy, but they can be found in your diet. The most common dietary stimulants are the caffeine or caffeine-like chemicals found in coffee, tea, many cola beverages, and chocolate.

In the last 10 years, herbal stimulants have found their way into our diets, especially the diets of children, adolescents, and young adults. There has been a significant increase in the use of herbal "energy drinks," which contain stimulants such as guarana, gotu kola, ginseng, and yohimbine. These herbal stimulants have an effect similar to that of caffeine. They have become very popular with adolescents and young adults, because in moderate quantities they increase energy and endurance, and can aid in concentration. The problem is that these stimulants are sometimes overused and even abused. As a result, they might be associated with anxiety, hyperactivity, difficulty sleeping, stomach problems, and even aggression. Some people develop headaches after they stop consuming these products.

Parents need to inform their children about the potential dangers of using stimulants and carefully monitor their use.

Natural Antioxidants

An *antioxidant* is a chemical or other substance that has the ability to slow down a process called *oxidation*. In simplistic terms, oxidation is the process of aging. In more technical terms, it is a chemical process that produces *free radicals*, which can damage cells. Oxidative processes have been associated with many human and animal diseases, including cancer and coronary artery disease. A common antioxidant family is the *polyphenols*, which are found in red wine, black tea, green tea, olive oil, white tea, chocolate, peanuts, and pomegranates.

REST/SLEEP

The third health-promoting factor in the pyramid is rest/sleep. The body repairs itself during periods of rest, especially sleep. In the case of children, the body actually grows during sleep. A common misconception is that children can go without sleep, but this is not true:

- Three-year-old children require about 10 hours of sleep at night and 2 hours of nap time during the day.
- Teenagers require 8 to 10 hours of sleep.
- College students require at least 8 hours of sleep.
- After 17 hours without sleep, a person has the reaction time of someone with a blood alcohol level of 0.05 percent; after 24 hours without sleep, the reaction time is similar to someone with a blood alcohol level of 0.1 percent, which is considered legally intoxicated in most states.

A lack of sleep interferes with your children's ability to learn, so it is common to see children who do not get adequate sleep doing poorly in school. More specifically, it is the lack of REM sleep (rapid eye movement sleep during dreaming) that is associated with the inability to remember things. Conversely, getting adequate REM sleep is associated with enhanced memory and creativity. REM intervals increase in duration near the end of the sleep cycle for most people, so waking up extra early to study or pulling an "all-nighter" might not be a good idea after all.

Lack of sleep is a major concern for children, so much so that Lawrence Epstein and Steven Mardon wrote an article entitled "Homeroom Zombies," which appeared in the September 17, 2007 issue of *Newsweek*. The article discussed the almost epidemic problem of inadequate sleep. They reported that some schools have gone so far as to move starting times from 7:15 a.m. to 8:40 a.m. Preliminary results revealed attendance increased, auto accidents decreased, and grades appeared to improve.

If you are wondering about us "older folks," we need 7 to 8 hours of sleep a night. But, I'll tell you a secret: I recently discovered "the nap." Yes, that afternoon departure from consciousness lasting 15 to 30 minutes. I used to think a nap was something old people or babies did, but one of my daughters saved me from this mistaken idea. One day, she said she was going to take a *nap*.

"A nap?" I said. "You take naps?"

"Yeah, dad—*power naps*."

Ah, the power nap. Yes, indeed, wording is everything!

If the "power nap" sounds good to you, there may even be a "super power nap"…*the relaxation response*. Dr. Herbert Benson authored a highly influential book in 1975 entitled *The Relaxation Response*, which reported on research showing that meditation and related practices were able to create a state that he termed "the relaxation response." His research and the work of others have shown that the relaxation response is not only the opposite of the classic "fight or flight" stress response, but prolonged practice can actually assist in the development of resistance to stress and a highly resilient mind and body. Now, couldn't we all use some relaxation, especially stressed-out children and young adults? Consider the following.

The human body begins to experience a variety of problems when it is overstimulated over a prolonged period of time, but the relaxation response can be the antidote. The regular practice of meditation, prayer, visual imagery, biofeedback, and even self-hypnosis, can be useful in helping people recover from stress-related illnesses to the degree to which the illness is truly stress-related. If this theory is correct, it means that we all—especially children—have an innate ability to resist stress-related disease and dysfunction, but that ability must be cultivated. Perhaps teaching this skill is our responsibility as parents.

Early in my clinical training, I was working with a patient who had unrelenting anxiety. I began teaching him techniques, such as meditation and deep breathing, designed to create the relaxation response. He was instructed to practice 15 to 20 minutes every day. After 6 weeks of diligent practice, he came into my office more upset than usual.

"Doc, I'm worried, he said. "In the last few days I've noticed that the things that used to bother don't bother me anymore! What's going on?"

I smiled and said, "You're getting better!"

HomeWork

Think about times when you've let yourself get into a stew about something. But, looking back at it now, you see that you were unnecessarily spinning your wheels. What about times when you did something—like maybe even just sitting down and taking a few deep breaths—and found that it helped you respond to a situation in a calmer manner?

Write about several situations in which you found a way to lower your stress level. Ask your children to identify similar situations in their lives and write about them. Then discuss what you've written and what you can do to create the relaxation response.

The effects he reported were similar to those of an antianxiety medication, but in his case he was not on medication—he was just creating the relaxation response. What more useful gift could we give our children than the innate ability to remain calm in the face of chaos?

ATTITUDE

As I mentioned earlier, the traditional health-related factors rest upon the most important element in the Health Promotion Pyramid—attitude. Attitude refers to the consistent manner in which you interpret the world around you, and the meanings that you assign to people and events in your life. It's how confident you are in yourself and your abilities. It's all of these things and more.

Throughout history the importance of attitude has been emphasized. Take a look at these quotes throughout history. What do they have in common? What message are they trying to send?

> *Men are disturbed, not by things, but the views which they take of them.*
> —Epictetus

> *It's not what happens to you that matters, but how you take it.*
> —Hans Selye

> *The mind is its own place and in itself can make a Heaven of a Hell, or a Hell of a Heaven.*
> —John Milton

> *For there are no things good nor bad, but thinking makes them so.*
> —William Shakespeare

Why is attitude so important for health and resiliency? Attitude is the difference between giving up and trying harder. It is the difference between listening to the "peer pressure" of friends and listening to the voice within you. It's the difference between eating what is good for you and eating what simply tastes good, but might not be healthy. It's the difference between going to the gym and going to the bar. It's the difference between doing what you know is wrong and doing what you know is right, even if it's harder. Attitude is the difference between taking what you need for yourself and giving to others.

Sounds good. But, my colleagues and I decided to see if it really works. We surveyed several thousand people in order to see which was the most important: the situations you find yourself in, or the way you choose to react to those situations. Our research findings were very interesting because they indicated that Epictetus and Selye were right! It's not *what* happens that distresses people; it's *how* they react to the events that happen to them and unfold around them.

More specifically, we found that stress-related physical illness, job satisfaction, "burnout," and the desire to quit your job were more related to your *attitude* toward the job than the job itself. This is an important and powerful finding. Why? Because it's empowering. It says that you are not a slave to your job or the world around you. It says that, although you cannot always choose *what* happens to you, you *can* choose how you *react* to it—and that's powerful—that's ATTITUDE!

For example, let's look again at suggestions on coping with loss of a person or a relationship. Focus upon the things *gained* from the relationship, NOT what was *lost* because the relationship is no longer there. Positive memories are things that can never be taken away, but negative thoughts and memories will plague you forever, if you let them. The choice is yours—and making that choice is part of attitude.

When I was about 23 years old, my fiancée and I were shopping in a department store. I noticed that a new book had come out: *Type A Behavior and Your Heart.* I started to read it right then and there. When my fiancée returned from doing her

HomeWork

When has your attitude about a personal situation negatively affected your health—actually made you sick? When has a positive attitude affected your life? Write down one experience for each. Ask your children to think about these questions and write their response, and then talk about what you've written.

shopping, I was excited to tell her that I had found a book that described me exactly: competitive, aggressive, always rushing, easily bored, always doing more than one thing at a time, and impulsive.

The author said the name for this type of person was *Type A*. My soon to be wife, a registered nurse, looked at the book, smiled, and said, "So, remember to take out a lot of life insurance."

"Why?" I said.

"Because this book says that you are going to have a heart attack before you reach age 55."

A few months later, I went for my yearly physical exam. The physician said my blood pressure was higher than it should be in a person my age. He asked if I was stressed out about anything.

"I'm always stressed out," I told him. "I work two jobs, go to school full time, and I'm getting married."

The doctor told me I needed to learn to manage my stress.

I took his advice and learned meditation, exercised consistently, and watched my diet. More importantly, I slowly began to change my views of what was meaningful in life. It wasn't easy, but my blood pressure came back to a healthier level, I learned to look forward to exercise, and my views on life changed in such a way that I no longer consider myself to be a Type A person. But, that transformation might be a topic for another book!

TEN THINGS YOU DO *NOT* WANT TO TEACH YOUR CHILDREN ABOUT HEALTH

This is our DO NOT do list. These attitudes and actions are *not* health-promoting—they are health-eroding:

- Be a perfectionist, never accept excellence.
- Never exercise!
- Remember, the glass is always half empty!
- Eat as much "fast food" as possible. Never eat breakfast.
- Blame all of your failures in life on your parents; your lack of friends; your coercive, unethical, money-grubbing, outsourcing, capitalistic boss; or the great conspiracy of the other political party.
- Accept responsibility for everything that goes right and nothing that goes wrong.
- Engage in an endless process of controlling everything and everyone, especially those people/things over which you have no actual control.
- Strive to sleep as little as possible!
- *NEVER* take vacations; if forced to do so, feel guilty.
- Seek out a routine: Sleep until you are hungry, eat until you are tired; use alcohol to relax and stimulants to get going.

OK, 'fess up. How many of those "Don'ts" do *you* really do?

Your challenge in putting a health promotion plan together for your children is to be consistent. Encourage each child to make one change at a time to improve her health. Choose a behavior that you think each child can accomplish. The key to success is creating a plan that is significant enough to improve health, without being so radical or intense that your child will reject it. Remember, long-tem consistency is more powerful than short-term intensity.

HomeWork

- Begin by being a good role model yourself. Maintain an atmosphere in which the pursuit of health and wellness are appreciated and encouraged as part of your family values
- **Exercise:**
- Try taking a *family walk* around the neighborhood or in a park with your kids. Not only is it good exercise, but it's a natural time to promote better communications with all family members. How about the entire family joining a health club? (Obviously, you should never start an exercise program without clearance from your physician.)
- **Rest/Sleep:**
- Getting enough rest can be a challenge. This is true for all of us, not just children. I remember attending primary school. The part of the day I hated the most was nap time. Forcing children to rest might not always be a good idea, but there are things parents can do to help children get adequate rest/sleep:

-Limit caffeine consumption, especially 2 to 3 hours prior to bedtime.

-Strict enforcement of a standard bedtime schedule or routine is important.

-Encourage naps as appropriate, but they should be less than 60 minutes in duration and not after dinner, otherwise they might interfere with the natural nighttime sleep cycle.

-Be on the lookout for sleep disorders in your children.

- **Relaxation Techniques:**
- Many people who learn to meditate quit within a year of starting. Many of them say it's boring. In trying these techniques with your children, you might consider methods that are more active, compared to passive mantra-based meditations. Visualization and active muscle relaxation techniques might be more engaging for children.
- The active muscle method of relaxation involves closing your eyes while sitting or lying quietly, and then tensing and relaxing each part of the body, one after the other. You can start with your feet and work your way up your body slowly.
- Visualization exercises can also be effective. Think about taking 10 minutes, closing your eyes, and imagining yourself at some beautiful and relaxing place. If you choose the seashore, for example, try to imagine the sounds of the waves hitting the beach, the feel of warm breezes, even the smell of salt air. Think of this type of exercise as a mini-vacation without ever leaving home.

- Attitude: Children need to understand that events set the "stage" for our lives, but the way we respond (attitude) determines how each "act" is played out. Yogi Berra is credited with once saying that, when you get to the fork in the road, take it. To me this means that when you get to a decision point in your life, you have a choice. While you may not be able to change the event, you can change how you react…teach this lesson to your children by discussing the choices they have regarding how they can react, even when bad things happen. This will help reduce the stress potentially associated with the fear of poor performance.

Part Two:

BELIEFS TO
PROMOTE RESILIENCY

Beliefs are judgments, expectations,
or forms of acceptance

Learn the Power of Optimism

OPTIMISM IS THE TENDENCY TO TAKE the most positive or hopeful view of life. It means expecting the best outcome, and it's the belief that good prevails over evil. Optimistic people are more resilient than pessimists. Let's take a closer look at optimism.

POLLYANNA AND THE GLAD GAME

Did you ever read the story of Pollyanna? *Pollyanna, The Glad Book* is a classic children's book, written in 1913, by Eleanor H. Porter. It tells the story of Pollyanna Whittier, a young girl who goes to live with her Aunt Polly after the death of her father. As you can guess from the subtitle, *The Glad Book*, it's about optimism and positive attitudes. The book was made into a Walt Disney movie in 1960 starring Hayley Mills. In both the book and the movie, Pollyanna is portrayed as a very upbeat and optimistic girl, despite the tragic loss of her father.

How did Pollyanna remain so optimistic? Whenever unfortunate things happened,

If you can imagine it, you can achieve it. If you can dream it, you can become it.
—WILLIAM ARTHUR WARD

Pollyanna would play "The Glad Game," a game that her father had taught her. Let me quote from the book:

> *Nancy the household maid says to Pollyanna one day, "You don't seem ter see any trouble bein' glad about everythin'."*
> *Pollyanna laughed softly.*
> *"Well, that's just the game...Father told it to me, and its lovely," rejoined Pollyanna.*
> *"The—game?"*
> *"Yes; the 'just being glad game'...the game was to just find something about everything to be glad about—no matter what t'was," rejoined Pollyanna earnestly.*

> *The measure of mental health is the disposition to find good everywhere.*
> –RALPH WALDO EMERSON

In the book, Pollyanna is described as a young lady who has an unquenchable thirst for the positive things in life. When I think about it, that's a rather enviable perspective to have. What a wonderful gift it would be!

Unfortunately, over the years, the name *Pollyanna* has come to mean someone who is distracted by wishful, naïve, and unrealistic thinking (some pessimist probably said this). However, Pollyanna was not naïve—she was optimistic, and that's something we want our children to be, isn't it? I hope my children learn how to see the "silver lining" in every cloud. Keep in mind, however, that optimism should never blind us to the sometimes unpleasant realities of the world in which we live.

WHAT IS OPTIMISM?

According to Dr. Martin Seligman, a noted researcher on the subject, optimistic people are different from pessimistic people in three ways. They get depressed less often, they are higher achievers, and they are physically healthier than pessimistic people.

An optimist is a person who maintains a positive view of the world, expects positive things in life, and is generally very hopeful. Optimism is the opposite of pessimism. When asked the classic question, "Is the glass half full or half empty?" the optimist says the glass is always half full, while the pessimist says the glass is always half empty. Which do you want your child to be?

HomeWork

Time for a little self-examination. Are you a half-empty or half-full kind of person? How do you know? How do you see that reflected in your children's attitudes?

Pessimism is associated with an increased incidence of depression. Optimism might provide our children (and us, too) with psychological immunity against depression. In his highly recommended book, *The Optimistic Child*, Dr. Seligman makes the case that depression is a virtual epidemic that has gradually increased over the years, to the point at which, in one study, the incidence of a depressive disorder in adolescents was 9 percent. Prior to 1960, depression was relatively rare, reported mostly by middle-aged women. Now it occurs in both males and females as early as middle school, and its prevalence increases with age.

Dr. Seligman argues that social change is at the root of this epidemic, and that it breeds pessimism and depression. These changes can be seen as a shift in social goals as well as a shift in orientation.

Our society has changed from an achieving society to a feel-good society. Up until the 1960s, achievement was the most important goal to instill in our children. This goal was overtaken by the twin goals of happiness and self-esteem…. self-esteem is caused by…successes and failures in the world …[what we need] is not children who are encouraged to feel good, but children who are taught the skills of doing well.
–DR. MARTIN SELIGMAN

As Dr. Seligman points out, self-esteem is needed in order to be truly happy. Obviously, there is nothing wrong with self-esteem and happiness, as long as they are based on a foundation of something more substantial than the mere desire to possess them, or the desire to give them to our children.

Remember the discussion about my daughter, who was given trophies for just showing up? I wonder if a shelf full of trophies really helped her self-esteem, her optimism, and her belief in herself? The concept of unmerited compliments comes into play here, too. If we provide our children with encouragement to succeed without the *opportunity* to succeed and—yes—even to fail, we will have offered them a sense of well-being that is superficial and short-lived. Self-esteem based on empty compliments erodes with time, especially if put to the test in a competitive, and sometimes hostile, world.

As for orientation, Seligman believes that we have seen a shift from teaching children the value of affiliation with things greater than themselves (commitment, duty, family, community, nation, and God), to teaching them that the most important thing in life is personal happiness, an entitled focus upon "oneself," regardless of what it costs others. As these children grow into adults, we can predict the emergence of a generation of selfish, self-centered adults who are unable to take responsibility for their actions and persevere in difficult times, and who easily quit jobs, friendships, and marriages with minimal hesitation or regret when those situations become challenging or do not lead to "true happiness."

HomeWork

How and when do you compliment and praise your kids? Which do you emphasize more often to your children?

- *Doing* something that will make you happy is important, *or*
- Just being happy is important.

How is that reflected in their own expectations of life?

SELF-FULFILLING PROPHECY

A self-fulfilling prophecy is a prediction that increases the likelihood it will come true by the very act of making it. Sociologist Robert Merton coined the term in 1949, in his book *Social Theory and Social Structure*. It seems to work by virtue of the fact that, if you expect to behave in a certain manner, you start to think a lot about it, and that focus seems to actually change your behavior.

For example, I was playing golf the other day. All I had to do was hit the ball about 150 yards over a pond, which is a shot that I can make easily. I took out an old golf ball to hit rather than the ball I had been playing. My friend asked why I switched golf balls before I teed off. I said I did not want to lose a new golf ball in case I hit the ball into the water. Well, guess what? I hit the ball right into the water. My friend laughed and said that the reason I lost the ball was because I *expected* to lose it. He said he always looks at the golf green and imagines the ball landing close to the target. By picturing success, he relaxes as he hits the ball. Because I worried about losing the ball in the water, my body became tense, my swing was altered, and my expectation was fulfilled.

> The ultimate function of prophecy is not to tell the future, but to make it.
> –W.W. Wagar

Although Robert Merton coined the term "self-fulfilling prophecy," it was Russell Jones who compiled a remarkable review of the phenomenon in his 1977 book *Self-fulfilling Prophecies*. Case after case seems to suggest that, if you devalue yourself, you are likely to attain a devalued outcome at home, at school, on the job, and generally in your life. On the other hand, if you value yourself, you are more likely to achieve a positive, valued outcome.

> Researchers…have known for years that if, in a given situation, individuals devalue themselves… this perception will virtually ensure failure… The converse of this relationship is true as well. If you imagine yourself succeeding at your task, your probability of success will be greatly enhanced.
> –Daniel Girdano

Optimists tend to value themselves and everything they do, while pessimists devalue themselves and their actions. Who will be happier? Who is likely to be more successful? That's right—the optimists. Basically, optimists tend to benefit from the self-fulfilling prophecy phenomenon—and, by virtue of that benefit, it's actually easier to be an optimist!

HOW DO WE HELP OUR CHILDREN BECOME OPTIMISTIC?

The key to helping our children become optimistic can be found in the beliefs that they hold about themselves and the world in which they live. Dr. Seligman has shown that people can be taught optimistic behaviors, and he suggests that optimistic people think differently from pessimistic people in three ways:

- Optimistic people see problems as temporary rather than as long-lasting.
- Optimistic people see problems as being specific and limited in scope, rather than general and pervasive.
- Optimistic people recognize that many of the things that go wrong are beyond their control. As a result, they do not blame themselves needlessly—a tendency that many pessimistic people indulge in.

Dr. Albert Bandura has studied ways to increase a person's sense of what he calls *self-efficacy*. His work is summarized in his writings: *Self-efficacy: The Exercise of Control.* Dr. Bandura defines self-efficacy as the belief in your ability to exercise control in a meaningful and positive way. More specifically, self-efficacy is a belief in your ability to organize and execute the actions required to achieve necessary and desired goals. A more current phrase that expresses the same thing is "believe in yourself." This perception of control, or influence, is an essential aspect of life itself. If you believe that you can accomplish what you set out to do, you will improve your chances of success, and you will have less stress.

People guide their lives by their beliefs of personal efficacy.… People's beliefs in their efficacy have diverse effects. Such beliefs influence the courses of action people choose to pursue, how much effort they put forth in given endeavors, how long they will persevere in the face of obstacles and failures, their resilience to adversity, whether their thought patterns are self-hindering or self-aiding, how much stress and depression they experience in coping with taxing environmental demands, and the level of accomplishments they realize.

–Dr. Albert Bandura

Dr. Bandura says that there are several ways to build self-efficacy and optimism, which, in turn, help build stress-resilience. The most powerful way is by experiencing success, or *enactive attainments*. Success raises your belief in yourself and makes you more optimistic—repeated failures lower your belief in yourself and lead to pessimism.

What is most amazing is that achieving success is all in the eye of the beholder. That is to say, *objective success won't help your self-efficacy or build optimism if you perceive your success as a failure.* Let's use the experience of the United States in the Vietnam conflict as an example. As the perception of efficacy eroded, so did political support. Objective military success was subordinated to the perception that this was a "war that could never be won," and retreat became the only option.

Another way to increase self-efficacy and optimism is through vicarious experiences. If you watch someone similar to yourself succeed at something, you are more likely to be optimistic about your own ability to succeed. If, on the other hand, you watch

HomeWork

Ask your children who made this statement, an optimist or a pessimist?

"If you see light at the end of a tunnel, its likely to be an oncoming train."

If they said an optimist, they're wrong. If they said a realistic, they missed the point completely, and you have your work cut out for you! The quote comes from Robert Lowell and is what a "glass-half-empty" pessimist would say.

someone similar to yourself fail at something, you are more likely to be pessimistic about your ability to succeed.

Verbal encouragement and personal support increase optimism and self-efficacy. Verbal encouragement includes such things such as suggestions, education, and reinterpretation of experiences (pointing out that the glass is half full rather than half empty). Finally, physical and emotional reactions can shape self-efficacy.

MOVING ON DESPITE ADVERSITY

A patient who had been diagnosed with terminal cancer came to me for assistance in "getting her life in order" before she died. This 32-year-old woman had been given 6 months to live. She asked me to help her "get ready to die." After I reviewed her medical records and listened to her story, I simply replied, "I'm sorry, I do not get people ready for death, but I will help you live each day as meaningfully as you can whether it's for 6 moths, 6 years, or 60 years."

We talked about attempting to remedy any regrets and mend strained friendships. Most importantly, we talked about looking forward and being as optimistic as possible. I taught her relaxation and pain management techniques that helped reduce her pain. Six months became seven. Seven months became 12. One year became two, and she is now in complete remission. Where there is life, there is hope. (I will say more about this in Lesson #6.) I'm not saying that being optimistic can absolutely

People rely partly on their state of physiologic arousal in judging their capabilities and vulnerability to stress. Because unusually high [stress] arousal usually debilitates performance, individuals are more likely to expect success when they are not beset by aversive arousal. Fear reactions generate further fear through anticipatory self-arousal.... People can rouse themselves to elevated levels of distress that produce the very dysfunctions they fear.

–Dr. Albert Bandura

cure terminal illness, but it can make the journey more tolerable, whatever the final outcome, as the next example underscores.

A surgeon asked me to see one of his patients who was suffering from advanced heart disease and desperately needed a heart transplant. The patient was severely depressed, which further worsened his prognosis. The surgeon asked if I could be of assistance while the patient waited for a donor heart for transplantation.

James was 47 years old, but he looked much older. He had suffered an illness that had affected his heart in such a way that it no longer functioned effectively. James' wife was angry and resentful. On one occasion, she actually awakened him and said, "Aren't you dead, yet? I wish you would just die and get it over with!"

James was angry, but mostly he felt betrayed.

My work with James was to help him learn the art of living in the moment, while at the same time looking forward to the next moment. We talked about learning to appreciate the things people often take for granted. I encouraged him to begin writing a journal, not just of daily events, but about the lessons he had learned throughout his life. I asked him to contact old friends with hopes of renewing those friendships, via letters, if not in person. These things were done not as a way of "getting his house in order," but rather as a way of building a platform for the next phase of his life.

I received a call on a Monday evening from his 25-year-old daughter. I typically saw James on Tuesdays. She said that her father had died in his sleep on Sunday night. As I was expressing my condolences, she interrupted me and said, "My father's prognosis was poor, and he knew that. But in the last few weeks his mood and the quality of his life was greatly improved. Thank you."

You might think that this story had an unhappy ending. You might ask what does it have to do with optimism—even though James was optimistic, he still died. No one is guaranteed a future;

our only guarantee is the present. You can choose to lament the uncertainty of life or celebrate the gift of the moment with an eye toward the future. Regardless of the future, I believe that such an optimistic perspective improves the quality of life for the moment—and what is life anyway but a series of moments?

HomeWork

1. Are you a half-empty or half-full kind of person? How do you know? How do you see this attitude reflected in your children? Talk with your kids about this concept, and ask them to write about an experience in which they or someone they know saw the "glass as half empty" or "half full." Write about your own experience, and when everyone is finished writing, talk about what you've written.

2. How and when do you praise your kids? Which do you emphasize more often to your children: praise or criticism? Talk with your kids about the last time someone (including you) praised or criticized them. Ask them how it made them feel.

3. Self-esteem and optimism are built on success (attaining goals), not just encouragement. Create opportunities for your children to succeed. Help them choose realistic goals that build on one another, so that a small success leads to larger ones. Ask your kids how you can help them set and reach goals that will make them feel good about themselves.

Encourage your children to attempt challenges they might not choose on their own. Help them do their best. Encourage them to try again, even if they fail. Before attempting a challenge, have your children watch other children successfully doing the same things they want to achieve—this is called *vicarious attainment.*

4. Encourage your children to keep a journal. This is one of the most amazing tools a child can use, yet it is underused, especially by boys. Written expression serves to reduce stress and reduce frustration, and it encourages a calm and rational analysis of situations.
5. Every night before going to bed, have your children talk about and write one thing they each look forward to the next day.

The Importance of Faith

WHAT IS FAITH?

Technically speaking, faith is an expectation or belief in something for which we might have no tangible, objective evidence. Psychologically, faith allows us to accept the things we cannot understand. It provides meaning to our lives and the world we live in. It's a form of psychological *glue* that holds all of our experiences together and puts them into context. Faith allows children and adults to derive a sense of order in the world. This sense of order has been referred to as a *sense of coherency.*

With faith, there are no mysteries, only answers yet to be revealed. Faith will allow your children to sleep well, even when the world appears out of control. We often think of faith in terms of religious faith, but faith is not restricted to formal religion. You can have faith in science, philosophy, justice, and spirituality that is not based on a specific ideology. Faith fuels optimism. The sun will rise in the morning, and we have the choice to welcome each day full of hope and optimism—or riddled with pessimism,

Faith is that which allows us to accept the things we cannot understand. Faith is believing that the challenge in front of you is never as great as the power behind you.

regret, and despair. Teach your children that the choice is theirs to make.

Some pragmatists criticize faith as being irrational because it might not be based on observable, objective data. The flaw in this argument is that it assumes science has the capability to reveal all the "mysteries of the universe," and that science is never wrong. Scientists have been wrong in the past, and they will continue to make mistakes in the future. Almost all new discoveries are based on faith in something not yet observed or demonstrated. Here is a story to illustrate how faith and optimism work for some people:

When I was in Scandinavia during a very cold winter doing training with rescue personnel, a priest asked if I could speak with one of his parishioners, a man he was worried about. He said it would be brief, because the man, Olaf, wanted to ask me just one question. I agreed to meet them for lunch.

Olaf was very large, about 6'6" tall and 260 pounds. He approached the table with marked hesitation, unable to look me in the eyes. I asked him how I could help him.

"Two years ago my village was hit by an avalanche," he said. "Many homes were covered by ice and snow. The first home I dug out was my own, and the first two bodies I recovered were those of my two sons, 6 and 4 years old."

At this point, tears streamed down Olaf's face, literally falling into his soup. He raised his head and finally looked at me, and then continued, "I will ask you only one question: Can you help me? Every day is a burden…I miss my sons so much that sometimes it hurts to breathe."

At that moment, I felt saddened and a bit overwhelmed. As a father, I could not imagine the pain Olaf must be experiencing. I thought for a few moments, and then said, "Tell me about your children."

Olaf beamed. He said they were wonderful boys, mischievous and a lot like him. He told me about their hobbies and how much they enjoyed fishing, even at that young age.

Then I asked another question, "Where are your children now?"

Olaf looked confused for a moment; then he smiled and said, "My boys are in heaven."

"Tell me about heaven," I said.

"Heaven is a wonderful place, a place where all good souls go. My wife and I live our lives so that we will be there someday."

"Tell me how you know this," I said.

"I know because I have faith in scripture, in my priest, and in God."

I thought for a moment and smiled. "So your family will be reunited someday," I said. "You and your wife will see your sons again, but this time it will be in heaven, and it will be forever."

When Olaf left the table, he seemed to be a different man from the one who had come to ask me "one question." He simply needed to be reminded of the powerful gift he had been given: *the power of faith*. In this case, faith meant accepting what he could not understand, even when it was so painful, but with an expectation that there is a "grand plan" in life that is a source of hope for the future. Whether we understand it or not, faith means that life is moving along as it should.

I returned two years later and saw Olaf's priest again. I asked about Olaf and his wife. The priest smiled. "Olaf, his wife, and their new infant daughter are all doing very well," he said.

FAITH AND MEANING

Another way of looking at faith is that it is a set of assumptions.

Dr. Viktor Frankl, a concentration camp survivor, wrote that the failure to find meaning and a sense of responsibility in one's life

He who has a why to live can bear with almost any how.
—FREDERICK NIETZSCHE

lies at the root of mental illness and behavioral problems. Frankl explained that people who lose the *why* to live also might lose the *how* to live.

Faith can bring meaning and understanding to our lives. In doing so, it reduces anxiety and brings a sense of comfort during stressful times.

Children are continually searching for meaning. They want to make sense of their world—they need to feel that they have some control over their lives. But, mostly children need to have trust in those who care for them. Lack of trust makes the world intolerable. It's not uncommon to see children who are neglected and abused actually make excuses for the adults who neglect or abuse them, especially if they need to rely on those adults for continued

Faithless is he who says farewell when the road darkens.
– J.R.R. TOLKIEN

care. They cannot tolerate the thought that the adults who care for them are mean, evil, or irrational. Sometimes, children will even blame themselves as a way to understand their circumstances.

THE POWER OF FAITH

Most of the research on faith has been focused on religious faith. You will probably find the results of this type of research fascinating whether you are spiritually inclined or not.

In 1996, cardiologist Dr. Herbert Benson wrote about what he called the *faith factor*, which is a combination of prayer or meditation and a deeply held set of philosophical, spiritual, or religious convictions. He suggests that faith-related practices, such as religious rituals and meditation, when practiced in childhood, may actually have the potential to lead to brain changes related to well-being in later adulthood.

Benson further suggests that belief in a *supreme being*—in whatever transcendent form an individual might choose to accept it—can be an influential source of strength and healing. Potentially, therapeutic effects associated with faith and faith-related practices include finding a sense of meaning, adopting a healthier lifestyle, and providing a sense of control.

Dr. Harold Koenig, of Duke University Medical Center, has argued that spiritual/religious beliefs can provide a sense of control over one's destiny and that, when a person puts complete trust in a personal deity and asks for forgiveness, a sense of relief and lowered stress is experienced.

Research has shown that people who use spirituality/religion as an end in itself seem to do better emotionally than those who use spirituality/religion as a means to achieving some other end, such as obtaining some tangible outcome. In that sense, faith can be like an overarching philosophy of life.

Faith-based practices appear to reduce alcohol, cigarette, and drug use, as well as improve quality of life measures for people suffering from cancer. Researchers at Duke University Medical Center revealed that 40 percent of patients ranked religion as the most important factor that enabled them to cope with the stress of being sick.

There is no sin or mistake in life that cannot be confessed and forgiven. Thus, no matter what a person has done in the past, he or she can start fresh again by recommitting one's life to God. Guilt, which religion itself can provoke, is erased by the simple act of asking for forgiveness. Not surprisingly, such beliefs may have powerful psychological consequences, and may indeed bring comfort to those who are lonely anxious, discouraged, or feeling out of control.

–Dr. Harold Koenig

Faith is closely aligned with optimism, in that it can serve our children by providing an overarching sense of order to the events in their lives, rather than simply seeing them as a series of random events. Faith sets the foundation for hope in the future, which is an essential ingredient for a healthy, happy life.

HomeWork

Here are some conversations and activities for you and your children that can bring focus and understanding to the concepts discussed in Lesson #6 and help kids develop faith in positive life outcomes:

- Children are naturally inquisitive and have a thirst for knowledge and understanding. Encourage them to read a wide variety of books that teach concepts beyond the tangible. Teach your children that they are a part of something greater than themselves. If they are exposed to different concepts, philosophies, and spiritual paths, they will naturally develop their own sense of meaning. But be prepared to answer some difficult questions!
- Read to your children beginning at an early age. Stimulate a thirst for knowledge and understanding.
- Provide books and other media that challenge your children to think about the concepts discussed in this Lesson. This web site: www.spiritualcinemacircle.com is a good source of movies designed to encourage contemplation of philosophical and spiritual concepts. Other Web sites with a variety of suggestions include: www.SpiritualityandHealth.com and www.beliefnet.com.

- Encourage your children to join organizations and interest groups through schools, houses of worship, or government-sponsored organizations that stimulate thought regarding philosophy, faith, religion, existentialism, and other constructs that help them see a "bigger picture."
- Perhaps teaching children to be part of something bigger than themselves begins with being part of a family, whatever that word may mean. Establish family routines and rituals that bring people together and encourage interaction: family dinners, even once a week; holiday rituals; birthday rituals; religious practices; sharing hobbies—you get the point. I learned to ride horses in order to spend time with my eldest daughter. I coached my children's sports teams. I learned to play golf in order to spend time with my son. Got it?

I have been a student my whole life. The second most powerful gift a student can acquire is the gift of asking questions. The *most* powerful gift a student can acquire is the understanding that not all questions have concrete observable answers. At some point, most children will then understand that there must be some other explanation...perhaps it can be found in this thing we are calling faith...faith in something greater than ourselves.

Part Three:

CODES TO PROMOTE RESILIENCY

*Codes are overarching sets of principles
or rules that ultimately serve
to guide all of one's actions*

Follow a Moral Compass and Cultivate Integrity

W E'VE SAVED THE BEST—or at least the most important—for last. Remember that the "C" in A-B-C stands for *Code*. As we defined it, a code refers to an overarching set of principles or rules that ultimately serve to guide all of a person's actions. Think of the code as the *glue* that holds together everything we've talked about up to this point. The code for true resiliency is integrity. Let's take a closer look at this seventh and final lesson on how to raise a resilient child.

The cover story in *Newsweek* magazine on February 12th, 2007, discussed a virtual epidemic of bad behavior by celebrities, who are often seen as role models. It posed the question: "[Is this a] coarsening of the culture and a devaluation of sex, love, and lasting commitment?" The authors did offer some hope: "Experts say attentive parents, strong teachers, and nice friends are an excellent counterbalance to our increasingly sleazy culture."

If you live a life of integrity, when you look back, the reflection will be something you can enjoy endlessly.
—ADAPTED FROM THE WRITINGS OF THE DALAI LAMA

Most children begin life with a basic misconception that's ingrained in our culture: You will be happy only if you acquire certain things, such as cars, boats, and planes, and do certain things, such as get promotions, win at contests (even if you have to cheat in order to win), and travel the world. We inadvertently teach that happiness is an end-point; a pot of gold at the end of the rainbow. Our children follow our example and chase the elusive treasure known as *happiness* by relentlessly buying *things,* and perhaps even pursuing the type of *people* they hope will make them happy. Too often, however, they discover that they really cannot afford the things they purchased, and the friends they pursued so vigorously end up disappointing them and stifling their growth. Many people never quite attain the level of happiness they were told those belongings, people, or experiences would bring—or they end up thinking there was something they missed in life. This could be called the "is this as good as it gets?" syndrome.

It seems to me that happiness is an ongoing journey, *not* a destination. If you live a life of integrity, when you look back, the reflection will be something you can be proud of and enjoy. A life without integrity easily becomes a life of excuses, negativity, and regret. A life lived without integrity is a life of selfishness that hurts others.

Better to fail with honor than succeed by fraud.
–SOPHOCLES

As they get older, will your children look back and see personal mistakes, failures, and carnage wrought upon innocent others—or will they basically live a life of honesty and integrity, a life in which they left behind more goodness than they took away?

How do you prepare your children for life? No veteran explorer would ever think of going anywhere without a compass. *You can give your child a compass—a moral compass called integrity.*

WHAT IS INTEGRITY?

Having integrity means being honest and adopting high moral principles. Simply put, integrity is the quality of doing that which is right.

It is doing what is good for you, and for others as well. Integrity isn't just a situation-by-situation process of decision-making; it's a consistent way of living. It's a personality trait our kids should have.

In 1967, Thomas Harris wrote the book *I'm OK – You're OK*, which was based on the work of Eric Berne. It became the top-seller of the 1960s and '70s. The book described the Transactional Analysis approach to understanding human behavior. Perhaps, although it offered valuable lessons and helped many people, it inadvertently caused some problems. The title alone allowed people to blur the distinction between right and wrong. Instead of helping people learn to stop beating up on themselves—going from "I'm a bad person" to "I'm OK"—a new attitude blossomed: "Anything I *do* is OK." Some of the twenty-first century's new rules seem to include:

- The end *does* justify the means.
- If it feels good, do it!
- Worry about it later.
- Do unto others before they do unto you.
- The person who dies with the most "toys" wins.
- Winning is not everything, it's the only thing.
- Morality is relative.
- We should not judge another's behavior.
- We are not really responsible for our actions.
- "The devil made me do it!" (a la comedian Flip Wilson).
- The ultimate marriage vows for the 1970s: "We take one another as husband and wife for as long as we both shall love."

We see this mindset at work every day, if not from people we know personally, then from those splashed across magazines, television, and the Internet. It makes arguing with your 8-year-old about unacceptable behavior even more difficult!

HomeWork

OK, be honest. Are any of those little dictums something you inadvertently subscribe to? What role models are you endorsing? What messages are you sending to your children?

The "anything goes" era of the 1970s and '80s spawned a plague of impulsiveness, insincerity, and irresponsibility, and—perhaps worse—duplicity. We have come to accept

A long habit of not thinking a thing wrong gives it a superficial appearance of being right.
–THOMAS PAINE

dishonest, immoral, and even illegal behavior from politicians, athletes, and entertainers. It's okay as long as the politicians vote the way we want them to, the athletes perform, and the entertainers entertain. These public figures become the role models for our kids. Parents, pay attention! What messages are you sending to your children? What role models are you endorsing?

Children must recognize that, contrary to what they see in the media, there really *are* a lot of rights and wrongs in our lives—more than we might wish to admit.

Let's look at the meaning of right and wrong:

- It is wrong to take something that is not yours or that has not been given to you.
- It is wrong to purposely hurt someone.
- It is wrong to lie to others for the purposes of hurting someone else or for helping yourself.

- A "half-truth" is still a lie if the intention is to deceive!
- It is wrong to withhold information if the intention is to deceive.
- It is wrong to cheat and take unfair advantage of others.
- It is wrong to betray a trust for the purposes of hurting someone else or for helping yourself.

Morality, like art, means drawing a line someplace.
—Oscar Wilde

Get it? Got it? Good. (Sorry, a little something I learned from my parents!)

A CLASH OF VALUES

How do you teach your child to have integrity? You make a choice as to what life lessons you're going to *both* practice and preach. So, what do you think? What matters the most?

- It's the *outcome* (or goal) that matters.
- It's the *process* (how you get there) that matters.

We have, in fact, two kinds of morality side by side: one which we preach but do not practice, and another which we practice but seldom preach.
—Bertrand Russell

As a society, we remain consumed with getting the *things* we want in life, without considering *how* we get them. It's only after we achieve those things that we begin to be plagued by the "how."

It boils down to that happiness thing, again. Happiness should be a result not of only *what* we have achieved (the outcome), but *how* we achieved it (the process). This includes *every* aspect of life. Hey, even Euripides in 450 B.C. had that one figured out.

Short is the joy that the guilty pleasure brings.
—Euripides

HomeWork

Think of your three greatest accomplishments. Did you achieve those things by honest effort, or did you bend the rules to attain them. Did you hurt someone else in the process? Did you even bother to think of the impact your actions would have on anyone other than yourself? How do you begin to teach your children integrity?

FOUR POINTS FOR YOUR CHILD'S MORAL COMPASS

Consider these four attributes as the four points of your child's moral compass:

- *Honesty.* Be honest. Tell the truth. Mean what you say. Say what you mean. Promises do not have expiration dates! Don't take unfair advantage (don't cheat). Don't take from others what is not yours.
- *Virtue.* The ancient Greeks thought of virtue in terms of fairness, morality, and ethical living. This also includes kindness. Be kind, always, no matter whether you win or lose. Expect to be treated as you treat others. When you can, without adversity to yourself, take care of others, especially those who cannot take care of themselves.
- *Self-discipline.* Within reason, hold yourself accountable for your actions. If you practice the first two points of honesty and virtue, self-discipline will be good for you and those around you.
- *Reflection.* Learn from your successes. Seek to repeat them. Learn from your mistakes. Be better because of them, not in spite of them!

Once the moral compass is in place, you'll know your child is pointed in the right direction: *to live with integrity*.

Not everything that came out of the 1970s and '80s was bad. How about this line from the television show, *Welcome Back, Kotter*, courtesy of Arnold Horshack? Teach your children to say "Winning is nice if you don't lose your integrity in the process" to themselves before taking a test, entering a contest, or playing a game or sport.

A PERSON OF INTEGRITY

Roger Staubach was born in 1942. He attended college at the U. S. Naval Academy, known for teaching the values of honesty and integrity. His unique attributes first emerged on a national level when he was selected to be the starting quarterback of the Navy's football team in 1962. He directed that team to a #2 national ranking, and earned the Heisman Trophy as the outstanding college football player of the year. Upon graduation from the Naval Academy, he could have left the military to play professional football, but he didn't. Not only did he decide to fulfill his military obligation, and thus jeopardize a potential career as a professional football player, he volunteered to serve in Vietnam.

> *To me, success is being able to feel good about how you've done things. You can't think only about, "What's in it for me?" You have to give back and try to contribute to the success of others. We want to win in business, but we want to do it right.*
> —Roger Staubach

In 1969, Staubach joined the Dallas Cowboys, as a 27-year-old rookie, to play professional football. He led them to four Super Bowl appearances, emerging as champions in Super Bowls VI and XII. He was named Most Valuable Player of Super Bowl VI, and he was named to the Pro Bowl six times during his 10-year NFL career.

> *It's all about integrity, values, and trust. If you have those attributes, and make sure your key people do too, there are no limits to what can be achieved.*
> —ROGER STAUBACH

In 1982, he formed The Staubach Company (TSC), a commercial real estate firm. In 2006, TSC reportedly completed $26 billion in commercial real estate sales.

How about your key people—your children? Do they have the attributes of integrity, values, and trust? This lesson is far too important to leave to luck. It's up to *you* to teach your children these attributes.

COMPANIES WITHOUT INTEGRITY: ENRON AND WORLDCOM?

Just as Roger Staubach's name is synonymous with integrity, the Enron Corporation has become synonymous with corporate fraud, deception, and corruption. Enron was an American energy company based in Houston, Texas, that clearly lived by the motto, "The end justifies the means." In late 2001, it filed for bankruptcy, after being one of the world's leading electricity, natural gas, and communications companies, with revenues claimed in excess of $100 billion in the year 2000.

What went wrong? The short answer is greed, arrogance, and dishonesty. Enron's meteoric rise as a shining example of American capitalism was fostered by accounting atrocities that included inflated profits, hidden losses, falsified accounting, and perhaps even political collusion. Enron reportedly formed a complex web of over 2,000 subsidiaries, almost 1,000 of them "off shore," in order to avoid U.S. governmental regulation and oversight. The scandal caused the dissolution of the Arthur Andersen accounting firm, one of the world's top five accounting companies. Enron's top executives, Kenneth Lay and Jeffrey Skilling, were convicted of fraud and conspiracy.

What Enron was to energy, WorldCom was to communication. WorldCom was one of the success stories of the 1990s. It grew into the largest Internet company and the second largest communications company in the world, employing over 60,000 employees in over 60 countries. Its power and wealth came largely from acquiring other companies. WorldCom revealed that it had incorrectly accounted for $3.8 billion in operating expenses and, on July 21, 2002, the company filed for Chapter 11 bankruptcy protection. However, rather than being a case of accounting errors, it was revealed that World-Com had intentionally committed fraud in order to inflate its stock prices by underreporting costs and inflating revenues.

CEO Bernie Ebbers became very wealthy from the stock that he held. However, he was forced to resign when questions arose concerning $366 million in personal loans that he obtained from the company. Mr. Ebbers was sentenced to a prison term for his role in the fraud.

CLOSING THOUGHTS

In a June 8, 2002 CNN/Money column entitled, "The Death of Confidence," Justin Lahart suggested that the WorldCom and Enron scandals might result in lasting harm to the U.S. financial markets and to investing in general. In the article, he wrote, "If trust in Corporate America was already broken, now it's in shambles. With that, many investors might decide to exit the U.S. stock market—and not come back." Similarly, Phil Ruffat of Mizuho Securities said, "We're seeing basically complete distrust in financial accounting in the Western Hemisphere."

In the case of Enron and WorldCom, and their respective corporate leaders now serving prison sentences, rather than the end justifying the means, perhaps we could say that in the end justice was finally applied to the means.

What happened? Someone forgot about integrity. Financial markets, friendships, marriages, and business relationships are built on confidence, trust, and integrity.

There can be no friendship without confidence, and no confidence without integrity.
—SAMUEL JOHNSON

What can children learn from these examples? I guess the lesson is that the stark absence of integrity in business, as well as in personal relationships, leaves a legacy of failure and regret. I also believe that conducting business and personal relationships with integrity brings a breath of fresh air, an ease—or even a joy—to these interactions. In an atmosphere of integrity, our children can learn to grow and reach their potentials rather than being concerned about "watching their backs," or when the other shoe is going to drop. In the "big picture," we should motivate our future leaders—our children—to a point at which they celebrate honesty and integrity, not because it is so rare, but because it is how we have learned to live as a society.

HomeWork

Here is our final list of suggestions for raising resilient children. What can you do to help your children develop a moral compass of integrity?

- As we said before, strive to be a role model for your children; practice what you preach. Your children will often follow your example. Even if they resist doing it, they will be quick to point out any contradictions between what you say and how you behave. Practice the four points on the compass of integrity, and your children will learn by your example:

- *Be honest.* Tell the truth. Mean what you say. Say what you mean. Promises do not have expiration dates! Don't take unfair advantage (don't cheat). Don't take from others what is not yours.
- *Fairness.* Play fair, work fairly, and be just. Many people might say that the world is not fair and just. This might seem true to many people, but it doesn't stop us from living as if it were true.
- *Kindness.* Be kind, always. Remember, your children are watching!
- *Reflect on your own actions* as a means of teaching your children to reflect on theirs. When you are successful, explain to your children why. When you are not as successful as you had hoped, explain the reasons. When you make a mistake, talk about it. Teach your children that there are valuable lessons to be learned from mistakes. Your goal is to make a habit of asking your children what lessons there are to be learned— win, lose, or draw.

  -Learn from others. When you see others acting in unethical ways or in a manner that lacks integrity, have the courage to point it out to your children. Don't simply ignore it!

  -*Make kindness a habit* that your children can observe and repeat. Find something kind to say about at least one person everyday. Maybe you could create another daily "game." Every day, your kids must perform a random act of kindness, maybe even anonymously. Ask your children if they know someone, another child or adult, whom they could help in some way.

-Remember Arnold Horshack, who said, "Winning is nice if you don't lose your integrity in the process." Teach your children to think about this attitude before taking a test, entering a contest, or playing a game or sport.

-As we said previously, give your children at least one compliment a day. Whenever possible, the compliment should be more about who they are, rather than something they have done.

Epilogue

We began this book with the assertion that every parent has the *obligation* to help children become stress-resilient. As I traveled the world and studied people who were resilient—and some who were not—I discovered that those who were resilient seemed to have an *inner strength* that made things possible. This inner strength is as simple as "A-B-C," which, to me, stands for the **ACTIONS**, **BELIEFS**, and **CODES** that form the core strength of personal character. Let me end this book as it was intended—as a gift for my children—a gift of the seven lessons of resiliency.

You have not lived today until you have done something for someone who can never repay you.

So, my children, Marideth, George, and Andi, this is what I have learned and what I hope you will learn about being resilient and about being a person of integrity.

Lesson #1: Seek friendships and mentors, recognize the value in others, and always show respect. Friendship is based on mutual trust, esteem, and—if necessary—an unhesitating willingness to offer support without any expectation that you will be repaid. Friends and family can often increase the joy of your successes and buffer the pain of disappointments.

Lesson #2: Be courageous. Learn to make the three most difficult types of decisions: win–win conflict resolution, loyalty, and when to struggle versus when to let go. As you approach a difficult decision, make the best decision you can and then let it go. The moment of absolute certainty will never arrive. If you must criticize, criticize the actions, not the person…that applies to yourself, as well.

Lesson #3: Take responsibility for your actions….this is shocking, I know! Taking responsibility for our actions is much easier when we realize that isolated actions, such as accidents and one-time misjudgments or miscalculations, are not *who* you are, they are simply *what* you did. Only when you know the outcome in advance, or repeat the same mistakes, are your actions a reflection of who you are.

Taking responsibility for your actions when things have not turned out well is not a sign of weakness, but rather a sign of strength and integrity. It's the recognition that no one is perfect. It *is* a statement about who you are, and it says you have integrity. It says you have courage and that you are concerned about people and things other than yourself.

Lesson #4: Invest in yourself; the best way to help others is to stay healthy. The best investment you can make is in your health. If you build a resilient body, your mind is more likely to be resilient, as well.

Lesson #5: Learn to be optimistic and accept the power of the self-fulfilling prophecy. The goal of prophecy is not to predict the future, but rather to *become* the future. Are you an optimist or a pessimist? What will happen in your future?

Lesson #6: Learn the power of faith. This will allow you to accept the things you cannot understand. With faith, there are no mysteries, only questions yet to be answered.

Lesson #7: Learn to follow a moral compass of integrity. Integrity is the "glue" that holds all of the other lessons in place—and don't forget the lessons of your grandparents, *The Greatest Generation*: Fidelity, Reliability, and Commitment, which can be translated into these five principles:

- If you give your word, follow through. Promises do not have expiration dates.
- Honesty is not the exception, it's the rule.
- Employment is a career, not just a job. An income is something you *earn*, it's not something you are *owed*.
- Take responsibility for your actions.

• Think about the consequences of your actions. They
affect others, always.

With love,
Dad

These lessons are the lessons I've learned. This, then, is my gift
to my children. I hope you will find it worthy of being a gift for
your children, too.

Index